AF505848

*The Spiritual Import
of Society*

THE SPIRITUAL IMPORT OF SOCIETY

John S. Connor, C.M.

VANTAGE PRESS
New York / Washington / Atlanta
Los Angeles / Chicago

Scripture texts used in this work are taken from the *New American Bible,* copyright © 1970, by the Confraternity of Christian Doctrine, Washington, D.C., and are used by permission of copyright owner. All rights reserved.

FIRST EDITION

All rights reserved, including the right of reproduction in whole or in part in any form.

Copyright © 1987 by John S. Connor, C.M.

Published by Vantage Press, Inc.
516 West 34th Street, New York, New York 10001

Manufactured in the United States of America
ISBN: 0-533-06881-9

Library of Congress Catalog Card No.: 85-91374

To Christ, the Lord:
the Way, the Truth, the Life.

Earnest expressions of gratitude are offered to:
the late Brother Alfred Grunenwald, F.S.C.,
Circulation and Resource Education Librarian,
La Salle University, Philadelphia, Pennsylvania,
and his alert assistants,
for their gracious and generous help
in my use of the library's excellent resources.

CONTENTS

PREFACE

This study's title has both an explicit and an implicit meaning. As presently stated it explicitly signifies the spirit's importance for society. Implicitly, though, it also signifies society's importance for human spiritual life. The two sides or aspects of the single theme obviously are complementary therefore. Emphasis is put on the spirit's significance presently, because our human condition's principal problems really exist in that vital area. While ample difficulties mark, and often mar, the societal order, such a reality at least receives extensive recognition and a relatively proportionate respect. The said recognition and respect includes influential professional scientists and philosophers, like the kind considered hereafter. Yet those same cultural leaders frequently fail to manifest a similar responsible reaction toward the spiritual components underlying and supporting, as well as mainly activating society. They thus partially accentuate, rather than alleviate, serious societal problems. Some excuse rightly should be allowed the latter, however, considering the bad example given them by certain prominent religious leaders. Belittling the intrinsic bonds between the natural and supernatural, hence likewise deflecting the due balance between the corporeal and spiritual, pseudoreformers actually encouraged excessive secular autonomy among scientists and philosophers. The resulting radical religious fragmentation further weakened traditional spiritual standards. Consequent upon these modern ''Western'' vital complications, the present study especially stresses human spiritual resources as society's crucial components.

Initial attention is addressed to the fundamental dynamic problem affecting human agents' spiritual awareness. It focuses chiefly on professional sociologists and philosophers with whom we are more closely connected during the following critical analyses. Their prominent cultural or educational impact largely compounds the basic difficulty that handicaps many if not most people, regarding spiritual consciousness and commitment. That confused condition entails extolling human nature's characteristic rational capacity, or reason (done verbally more often than vitally, as cloaking desire), at the expense of its prior, preparatory counterpart, faith. The eminence accorded the former, whether real or artificial, throughout our modern era since the alleged "Enlightenment," has correspondingly stimulated a strong assertiveness against the latter. As shown subsequently, human reasoning necessarily stems from faith, naturally or supernaturally, making the two dynamic traits inherently complementary, not contradictory. The posited opposition reflects cultivated preferences for a principally naturalistic, corporeally concentrated (consciously or unconsciously), spiritually subverted faith, sparking a supposed absolutely autonomous reason. This stands in contrast to a supernatural, truly spiritually enlightened faith, promoting a proportionately restrained or duly responsible reason. Society, being a spiritually integrated combination mainly, and its personal members, also mainly spiritually organized agents, have suffered serious setbacks that inevitably followed upon such pseudosophisticated corporeal exaltation.

As evidencing the compromised societal conceptions and commitments that the foregoing fallacious "enlightenment" has produced, the views of several more prominent contemporary social scientists and philosophers are compared. Although some differences, mostly marginal, concerning society's constitution distinguish these analysts, their overall outlook remains rather closely consistent. They typically manifest a corporeally bound awareness regarding reality, or at least regarding human cognitive ability to penetrate the same. Traditional, realistic rational enlightenment is then contrasted alongside the aforenoted modernistic, decidedly subjectivistic or rationalized kind. The former recognizes and reflects objectively given and garnered suprasensible or truly spiritual information, representing the contacted reality's substantive features. Such a vastly expanded and profoundly intensified, more typically reasonable cognitive consciousness, founded on supernatural faith, frees the thus temporally and spatially liberated (ultimately anyway) scientists and philosophers for fuller natural vital connections. It does so quite elementally, yet adequately fosters the conviction that further supernatural revelation remains possible and probable. Those enhanced insights and interpretations likewise provide rational objective standards assisting appropriate responses toward reasonably recognizable additional divine revelation.

After briefly reviewing the serious human structural imbalance on the corporeal side characterizing leading contemporary "Western" sociologists and philosophers, a summary survey of Oriental (Mongoloid) and African (Negroid) religious ideas and attitudes is offered. Both sharply contrasting types display a certain involvement with the supernatural, albeit along very fundamental lines. Mongoloid peoples' supernatural interest largely exhibits a highly theoretical, pronouncedly intuitive-reasonable approach. Its results resemble an ethical-philosophical system more than a religious one. Negroid peoples, on the other hand, show a stronger supernatural or a sharper religious attitude. It entails detailed, concrete, tangible practical, relatively instinctive-reasonable, moral-spiritual patterns. The two spiritual alternatives accordingly exemplify the effects of their limited, chiefly natural, inspirational sources. Spiritual values are heavily beclouded by corporeal counterparts: Mongoloids emphasizing the former in denying the latter, Negroids stressing the former and the latter almost synonymously.

Christian revelation is considered next, initially correlating it and the previously observed preliminary natural intimations affecting such advanced divine assistance. After noting the close consistency there, Christ's concentration upon spiritual control over corporeal is recognized as His messianic mission's crucial core. This basic human constitutional order critically supports a correspondingly concerted dynamic order. Such a substantive syndrome reflects the triple-tiered developmental system impregnating and activating human like all created beings. That predominantly spiritual linkage represents what traditional Christian theology denotes as the ''Trinitarian trace,'' or the divine creative impress. It was succinctly and significantly expressed when Christ outlined His salvific service to humanity as ''the way, the truth, and the life.''

Relationships between the three divine Persons comprising the Trinity are then summarily stated, derived from the aforesaid traditional theology. Those immanent interactions indicate the Persons' respective ''economic'' (creating) roles—ultimate sources of creation's triadic dynamism. Adequately viewed cosmically, they further indicate the second divine Person's closer connection with human creatures, as the second or middle creaturely class. This fundamental vital fact provides the basis for Christ's redemptive mission—the second divine Person humanly incarnate. It also underlies His emphasis on the middle term, truth, in His mediating message mentioned above. Thus personifying the mediative formal factor amid humans' essential dynamic equation (ends—final, means—formal, methods—functional), we see Christ stressing reform (spiritual over corporeal) as the central saving element.

Although Christian supernatural revelation's foregoing elemental features primarily affect human nature at the proportionately elemental personal-individual level, they carry additional, increasingly comprehensive social content. There we learn more truth about apt joint relations on the sexual, racial, and societal planes. The present study's considerations obviously must be limited to the last area. Here too we find a continuous consistent focus upon humanity's typical constitutional balance (spiritual over corporeal) as having crucial importance. Its impact consequently corrects the serious societal deficiency evidenced by the excessively naturalistic, corporeally concerned sociologists and philosophers noted earlier. Extending these insights into the societal realm, befitting an essential exigency, we then obtain a clearer and firmer systematized distinction between society's characteristic collective sectors. Such clarifications receive added enhancement when combined with similar supernaturally enlightened extensions of human beings' triple-tiered vital dynamism.

Viewing the so supernaturally inspired societal correlations and contrasts still more closely, on a theological-sociological scale, we see that they correspondingly intimate, intrinsically, Christ's fuller human import as the second divine Person made man. His mediating creative and redemptive role, between the first and third divine Persons, or formal Principle between final and functional Principles respectively, constitutes the common good that properly consolidates the several essential societal spheres. This common good, or the innate human capacities for personal-individual and societal-communal development, spawns and supports the various naturally inherent corporate constituents comprising society's organic outlines. It works chiefly along unifying, really spiritual lines, while simultaneously allowing, even advancing, proportionate corporeal diversity. The resulting real (not fictitious) entity, at whatever spatial and temporal level viewed (local, national, international), is a semisubstantial reality, possessing appropriate autonomous resources. Much like the personal members (individuals and groups), however, its control over constitutive elements remains limited.

Resembling personal constituencies also, an adequate or joint society exhibits combined spiritual and corporeal components. Those distinct, not separate, divisions display a similar basic dynamic pattern too, integrally interacting trialectically—as ends, means, and methods collectively. We thus discern religious, cultural (educational), and fine arts corporate units interrelating rather more spiritually. Political, familial, and mundane arts combinations do so somewhat more corporeally. Naturally, though, and supernaturally as well, the three typical dynamic models on each substantive side—spiritual and corporeal—react with one another more or less closely, as do their simpler counterparts on the personal-individual plane. The said trialectic traits likewise link up inside the several primary societal sectors. They entail planning, programming, and promoting, or continuous ends, means, and methods extensions. Such corporate roles are performed by aptly qualified persons, as the main substantive base for the entire system.

This study concludes while considering the additional sacramental supernatural relationships to Christ that revelation and the Church afford. These supply the spiritual power that Christians require for a proper practical response regarding the spiritual light flowing from the principles we previously examined. Adequately accepted and applied, then, both supernatural processes assure a proportionate participation, personally and societally, in the way and truth of eternal life.

John S. Connor, C.M.

St. Vincent's Seminary
Philadelphia, Pennsylvania

*The Spiritual Import
of Society*

Part I

Chapter One

THE BREAK BETWEEN MODERN FAITH AND TRADITIONAL FAITH

Despite their prestigious professional position, socially speaking, sociologists and social philosophers, with all the knowledge they possess, still resemble ordinary humans in one relevant respect. The imposing thought-full edifices erected by them, even as the countless humbler cognitive structures around them, are founded upon faith.[1] Like the latter, the former also must accept positive productive assistance from others, and much more than mere technical kinds, at the start of such ventures. Postulates or basic assumptions, partially objectively derived albeit variously subjectively modified, inevitably perform a crucial guiding role. Howsoever high they may eventually rise, human beings, as basically dependent learners, can only begin thinking by believing. Furthermore, although the original belief gradually may become transformed into real knowledge—through additional experience and reflection thereon—an element of faith (mystery or uncertainty regarding reality) always remains. The old adage is true: "One is never too old to learn," so long as he or she has the conscious capacity.

Sociologists normally admit this fact, if rather marginally and somewhat obliquely. Being modern scientists, hence firmly adhering to the "new morality of critical judgment that has seized the imagination of the scholar in the Western world,''[2]* they apparently experience professional embarrassment over such an admission. It does not fit well with the prime tenet in the said ''new morality,'' namely—''radical autonomy.''[3] Nevertheless, that attitude of fundamental dependence especially impinges upon the sociologists, since their science specifically stresses the individual's innate indebtedness to the group. Parsons accordingly acknowledges Weber, Durkheim, and Freud as his ''most important intellectual models.''[4] Sorokin similarly accepts guidance from Comte for foundational features characterizing his sociological analysis.[5] MacIver likewise explains his approach as following the example set by Weber and Mead mainly.[6]

Those initial dogmatic assumptions actually do not impose more than most elementary limitations on their recipients' autonomy. Beyond a belief in society as a reality *sui generis* (relatively), and a corresponding conviction that it chiefly entails functional processes largely contained within an historical-evolutionary dynamism, the so oriented scientists are free to make independent interpretations concerning the data observed. This is the professional claim anyway. A more objective appraisal uncovers additional hidden dogmas, however, and reaffirms the truth of another old adage: ''Be wary of one who gives testimony of himself.'' Again, the sociologists' scientifically established emphasis upon the profound influence that society exerts over the individual stimulates a strong skepticism regarding the radical independence alleged.

When we take a closer look at the ''new morality of critical judgment'' noted above, considering its central principles, we discover a yet deeper dogma providing the really revolutionary insight behind the attraction ''that has seized the imagination of the scholar in the Western world.'' Such principles include ''Autonomy, Assessment, and Sound Judgment.''[7] Obviously

* Reprinted from *The Historian and the Believer* by Van A. Harvey. Copyright © Van A. Harvey 1966. Used by permission of the Westminster Press.

there is nothing uniquely inspiring about them, since they represent traditional Western intellectual ideals. Their radical impact occurred only when these criteria were informed by the new way of looking at the world created by the sciences: ''when thinking for oneself meant thinking in terms of the new world picture; when rational assessment meant appealing to the known structures of present experience; when the quality of one's assent was seen to be a function of the warrants grounded in various areas of knowledge . . . thinking only became revolutionary when it was saturated by what we now call the common-sense view of the world.''[8] The ''scientific'' outlook or ''spirit,'' then, makes the crucial difference between traditional Western faith in individual autonomy, assessment, and sound judgment as compared with its modern counterpart. Both dogmatic attitudes demand belief, but a kind carrying decidedly contrary personal and social consequences.

In the Western world, before the ''scientific'' revolution, faith was principally objectively oriented, the historian Dawson tells us. People believed that reality reflected a given guiding order fundamentally. This basic pattern, divinely devised and decreed, constituted a foundation and framework, so to speak, which supported humans' more or less free efforts at self-development. The dominant vital theme stressed responsible, or duly deferential, concern for the whole community (collectively and individually), as equal fellow creatures. Membership bonds—whether on the local or larger, economic or cultural, professional or lay levels—were mainly spiritual or inner-centered (subjectively and objectively). They stemmed specifically from the intensive and extensive inspirational impact exerted by the Christian religion. The latter provided not simply a supernatural vision (faith) infinitely enhancing life's worth. It further supplied a concrete system—socially structured and culturally correlated (moral values and norms)—insuring the vision's gradual overt realization; if humans freely and fully, or historically and theologically complied therewith.[9]

Citing the testimony of the German theologian Friedrich Gogarten, Harvey states that "Luther's message shattered this understanding."[10] His dogmatic stand against the traditional Church's authority, even in the religious realm directly, had two results that profoundly facilitated the modern "scientific" attitude. By repudiating the latter's spiritual-moral dominion over the social order, he divorced life's natural and supernatural aspects. Similarly, through his emphasis upon what has become known as the "Protestant principle"—justification by faith alone, the way was opened for radical individual autonomy, supernaturally and naturally. "The upshot of this distinction between the two realms was to grant complete independence to the sciences," Harvey says. "In the name of faith, so to speak, science was free to do its own work."[11] That is to say the scientists could rightly concentrate on investigating reality from their natural viewpoint, without any consideration of possible religious or supernatural implications and complications. Since there are no objectively given guiding moral standards applicable here, the scientists properly devise them. Furthermore, through this reductionism regarding faith—a mere "trust in being itself" (God's goodness and salvific graciousness),[12] such belief could be interpreted as reflecting whatever scientists (physical-biological and human) discovered about the objects they studied. Thus, Harvey tells us, "the two elements of the morality of knowledge, autonomy and assessment, are but secularized versions of the ethic of faith."[13]

The great divorce that Luther inaugurated—drastically separating the supernatural and the natural, while likewise denying all formal social authority in religious affairs, implicity gave "full faith and credit" to humans' innate tendency toward aggressive self-assertion and a corresponding temporal insertion. Not only that, it also "sanctified" those attitudes if linked with a purely literal, hence actually lateral or most fundamental, supernatural faith.[14] His radical reduction, or elemental simplification, of Revelation's intent, content, and portent left any who followed him free for the various independent theological, philosophical, and scientific interpretations subsequently devised. Christianity consequently gradually splintered into countless competing, even mutually contradicting communities, distinguished from the traditional Church by their self-determined conception of biblical faith. Despite some exceptions at the basic moral level, the former became increasingly united against the latter, indirectly certainly, by their proportionately compromised stand on accepting "sophisticated" secular values and norms as constituting the modern meaning of that faith's moral implications.

The chief difference, then, between traditional and modern moral systems (concerning either knowledge or action) is found in the faith or belief underlying them. Traditional Christianity adheres to a divine Revelation, from above, authoritively assisting or enlightening humanity's efforts at moral development, naturally and supernaturally. Modern, relatively secularized, versions thereof dogmatically insist upon human discovery, from below, for authoritive guidance or enlightenment regarding mankind's moral progress, naturally and "supernaturally."[15]

MODERN ENLIGHTENMENT

Like so many modern "intellectuals," Harvey sees Immanuel Kant as the great exponent and expounder of this monumental movement. His key contribution was an essay explaining its chief characteristic—individual autonomy. Stated more exactly: he emphasized release by removing all restrictions on independent thinking.[16] "Have the courage to use your reason," he admonished; and obligingly formulated his own dogma, which would provide the foundation or faith that reasoning process requires. Kant adopted Hume's dogma, denying the mind's access to anything but sensible data. Through such a start, he confirmed and compounded the early epistemological revolt against the ages-old

Western view affirming humans' capacity for understanding reality's inner noumena, along with its outer phenomena.[17] Luther's great divorce (separating the spiritual and the temporal) can be seen influencing his follower Kant here.

Remarkably resembling Luther's exaltation of the individual's conscience as the autonomous principle linking the inner spiritual and the outer temporal realms, too, Kant devised the dogma that the mind's inherent categorizing or generalizing facility projected meaning upon sensible data. It has been named the "constructionist" approach, because the thinking subject believes he or she consciously constructs or organizes the relationships controlling objects contacted by the senses.[18] Under this theory, then, reality does not determine thought—except vicariously or sensibly. Rather, the thinker makes things real in the limited, temporally and spatially confined, way such subjectively slanted faith allows. Luther's dogma concerning moral justification, strictly through the individual's subjectively interpreted (hence actually accepted) faith, thus receives philosophical (subsequently scientific) extension from the "constructionist" dogma concerning human cognitional justification.

Kant's evident Lutheran import epistemologically was further unmistakably manifested when he expounded his moral doctrine based upon the categorically contrived, moral imperative dogma. Theoretically and practically considered, therefore, the Enlightenment's pioneer spokesman tellingly translated (consciously or unconsciously) the "Protestant principle" into scholarly secular terms. Gogarten consequently correctly sees the latter as making enlightened scientific autonomy possible.[19] Harvey also apparently recognizes close connections here: "Faith, as understood by the dialectical theologians, has a structure that, if it is not analogous to the new morality of knowledge, has a close affinity to it at many important points."[20] "Dialectical theologians" are those who, like Gogarten, sharply stress the Reformation's radical dichotomous impact at the most fundamental personal level. It not only established individual independence from ecclesial authority on the spiritual-moral plane, but similarly separated the subject's natural or worldly and supernatural or other-worldly concerns, as we have seen.

Kant's opting for limiting the objectively understandable order to reality's outer phenomenal realm prominently, if not perfectly, discloses what happens when professionals become captivated by their assumed autonomy. His epistemological doctrine reflected a move toward explaining the then new physics. He noted how the physical scientists experimented with things and accordingly discovered different general properties. In formulating the causal connection between the knowing subject and the known object, he could have applied (against expanding empiricism) the classical cognitional theory, which had long and largely influenced the Western world. Such a view held that the mind grasps the object's internal intelligible species, abstracting from the sensibly perceived external factors. Those generic and specific, or generalized and specialized qualities, representing the observed thing's substantive, integrative features (common among classes), proportionately impregnating and controlling its material components, activate humans' corresponding mental capacities concertedly. The resultant combined imaginative perceptions and intellectual conceptions enable the subject to reflect the object as a whole—substantially and supplementally, or spiritually and corporally. They thus produce both particular images and general-special categories within the mind. Insisting upon being autonomous, however, even exceptionally so through a reverential regard for reason—autonomy's assertedly absolute security—Kant took his cognitive ''cues'' solely from firm faith in his own.[21] Since this radically subjective fideism requires the strict rational conformity of the mind's judgments concerning reality, and its intrinsic categorical conceptualizations, if one expects ''objective'' understanding, supernatural elements are inadmissible unless they meet the requisite self-determined test. Revelation can be considered meaningful, therefore, merely as manifesting further human discernment or discovery.[22]

It is rather evident, then, why the Kantian epistemology has been adopted by many modernistic scientists, historians, philosophers, and theologians. Such a pronouncedly subjectivistic (humanly self-projecting) approach affords ample opportunities to devise allegedly reasonable, independent interpretations of reality. With no given, guiding values and norms recognized, other than what the said self-regulating agents commonly establish, those crucial vital standards ever remain almost entirely under humans' rationalizing dominion. Mutual agreement among the professionals involved (scholarly plausibility) becomes the ultimate validating criterion. Certainly the fact that the mind's conceptualizing and categorizing processes presumably follow axiomatic a priori laws, which basically influence our understanding's possibilities, sets some limits upon attempts at reconstruction and revision, theoretically anyway. Nevertheless, for their objectification, or practical implementation, these principles must be oriented toward empirical experience, if the so enlightened subjects would exercise a constructionist control over it.[23] When sensible data alone is accepted as the latter's content, and evolutionary change the chief characteristic thereof, the thus balanced believer can scarcely exempt more than minimal or fundamental cognitional and existential patterns from radical reformation. Modern enlightened faith accordingly achieves distinction by a "will-to-truth" based on a "will-to-believe" in mainly material: physical-biological, corporeal-psychological, criteria or warrants concretely considered. It has replaced so-called superstitious traditional faith—belief in the spiritual and the supernatural—as intrinsic to and ultimately determinative of the natural order, with a "substitious" or substitutional (corporeally and naturally determined) one (fallacy of misplaced concreteness).

Recalling Harvey's earlier statement regarding modern faith

being "informed by the new way of looking at the world created by the sciences,"[24] professional comments concerning this scientific viewpoint surely confirm the preceding critical observations. The physicist Einstein says,

> Physics treats directly only of sense experiences and of the "understanding" of their connection . . . the concept of the "real external world" . . . rests exclusively on sense impressions . . . the differentiation between sense impressions and representations is not possible. . . . Out of the multitude of our sense experiences we take, mentally and arbitrarily, certain repeatedly occurring complexes of sense impression . . . and we attribute to them a meaning. . . . Considered logically, this concept is not identical with the totality of sense impressions referred to; but it is an arbitrary creation of the human (or animal) mind. On the other hand, the concept owes its meaning and its justification exclusively to the totality of sense impressions which we associate with it.[25]

Jean Piaget speaks somewhat similarly as a psychologist when he tells us, ". . . intelligence is not a faculty . . . (it) is . . . only a generic term to indicate superior forms of organization or equilibrium of cognitive structurings . . . (it) involves a radical functional continuity between higher forms of thought and the whole mass of lower types of cognitive motor adaptation . . . its origins are indistinguishable from those of sensorimotor adaptation in general or even from those of biological adaptation."[26] The earlier American philosopher of pragmatism, John Dewey, believed that "Philosophy must go to school to the sciences; must have no data save such as it receives at their hands."[27] Consequent upon such schooling, he found thinking identical with most any kind of corporeal activity.[28]

As we have already noted, neither Kant nor his religious-minded, radically enlightened followers deny the existence of spiritual and supernatural realities. Because they believe absolutely in human reason's radical autonomy, however, and so see the natural order as its necessary operating sphere, understanding can be achieved only at the latter level; and solely through "rationally" conceived processes. The supernatural mainly represents the natural's further extension and elucidation for them, therefore. Similarly the spiritual is principally seen to facilitate the material or corporeal's fuller enhancement, by theoretically conceiving and morally controlling the constructive capacities inherent there. Kant's ideological ethical system precisely displays such belief's personal dynamic import.[29] Although admittedly very idealistic, and conceptually coherent, it ultimately constitutes a self-contrived and justified, as well as interpreted and applied, moral code (romanticism). Benefits and burdens, including obligations, are construed chiefly in subjective (self-serving) terms. Societal, like supernatural and spiritual, realities or relationships must be postulated (believed) and promoted, since they provide valuable supports enhancing the individual's temporal or natural existence.[30] This view, then, really reflects the philosophy of religion that Karl Rahner finds holding that "God is . . . the inner meaning and possibility of the world and the historical existence of man and no more."[31] It also believes "revelation . . . is simply the necessary complement of the nature of man himself," he says.

Thus the radical autonomy associated with modern enlightenment has produced several very significant results, from the theological standpoint. The Reformation's initial divorce between the natural and supernatural was gradually transformed into a new identification. The latter could only be discovered, or made credible certainly, through the former. Subsequently, with increased scientific and technical control over the natural (both human and physical), interest in the supernatural and the spiritual decreased proportionately. Amid the ensuing secularization, numerous new moral systems appeared, devised, legitimized, and institutionalized (more or less) by prevailing professionally plausible structures.

NOTES

1. H. B. Parkes, *Gods and Men: The Origins of Western Culture* (New York: Alfred R. Knopf, 1959), p. 473.

2. V. A. Harvey, *The Histtorian and the Believer* (New York: Macmillan, 1966), p. 38.

3. Ibid.

4. From *Social Systems and the Evolution of Action Theory* by Talcott Parsons. Copyright © 1977 by the Free Press, a division of Macmillan, Inc., p. 74.

5. P. A. Sorokin, *Society, Culture and Personality* (New York: Cooper Square Publishing, 1969), p. 17, note 28.

6. Robert MacIver, *On Society, Community and Power*, L. Bramson, ed. (Chicago: University of Chicago Press, 1970), p. 13.

7. Harvey, *Historian and Believer*, chapter 2.

8. Ibid., p. 68.

9. C. Dawson, *Religion and the Rise of Western Culture* (New York: Doubleday, 1958); see Introduction for summary. Cf. Harvey, *Historian and Believer*. Parkes, *Gods and Men*, p. 3ff. Barbara Ward, *Faith and Freedom* (New York: Doubleday, 1958), chapter 6.

10. F. Gorgarten, *The Reality of Faith,* C. Michalson et al., trans. (Philadelphia: Westminster Press, 1959), chapter 10. Cf. Ward, *Faith and Freedom,* chapter 8.

11. Harvey, *Historian and Believer*, p. 136.

12. Ibid.

13. Ibid., p. 138. (He cites Gogarten and his American counterpart, H. Richard Niebuhr, as agreeing on this.)

14. "The preacher shall preach only the Gospel rule and leave it to each man to follow his own conscience." See Ward, *Faith and Freedom*, p. 116.

15. "The heart of the issue before us is the collision of two moralities of knowledge, the one characteristic of the scholarly world since the Enlightenment, the other characteristic of traditional Christian belief."—Harvey, *Historian and Believer*, p. 127.

16. Immanuel Kant. "What is Enlightenment?" in *Critique of PracticaL Reason and other Writings in Moral Philosophy*, L. W. Beck, ed. (Chicago: University of Chicago Press, 1949), pp. 286–292.

17. Immanuel Kant, *The Critique of Pure Reason*, J. M. D. Meiklejohn, trans. of *Great Books*, volume 42, pp. 6, 23. See also Harvey, *Historian and Believer*, p. 39. (Kant's "will to truth" replacing traditional "will to believe.")

18. Meiklejohn, *Critique*, p. 23.

19. Gogarten, loc. cit.

20. Harvey, *Historian and Believer*, p. 135.

21. Immanuel Kant, *Metaphysical Foundations of Natural Science*, J.

Ellington, trans. (New York: Bobbs-Merrill Co., 1970), pp. 3–17; see also Translator's Introduction.

22. Immanuel Kant, *Lectures on Philosophical Theology*, A. W. Wood and G. M. Clark, trans. (Ithaca, N.Y.: Cornell University Press, 1978), pp. 160–164.

23. Ellington, *Metaphysical Foundations*. See also Translator's Introduction, and pp. 195–200.

24. Harvey, *Historian and Believer*, p. 68.

25. Albert Einstein, "Physics and Reality," *Journal of the Franklin Institute*, 221 (March 1936): 349–50. Excerpt reprinted by permission of The Franklin Institute.

26. Jean Piaget, *Psychology of Intelligence* (Totowa, N.J.: Littlefield Adams, 1976), pp. 6–7.

27. John Dewey, *The Influence of Darwin on Philosophy* (reprint ed., New York: P. Smith, 1951), p. 269.

28. John Dewey, *Experience and Nature* (Chicago: 1925), p. 67.

29. Immanuel Kant, *Lectures on Ethics*, L. Infield, trans. (London: Methuen, 1930), pp.36–47, 71–78. Cf. Wood and Clark, *Philosophical Theology*, pp. 40–42.

30. Ibid.

31. K. Rahner, *Hearers of the Word*, M. Richards, trans. (New York: Herder, 1969), p. 26.

Chapter Two

THE IMPACT OF MODERN FAITH ON SOCIOLOGY

SOCIOLOGICAL ENLIGHTENMENT

We noted at this study's start that the three contemporary sociologists mentioned there admit an authoritative allegiance to particularly prominent professional predecessors. Parsons acknowledges his basic dependence upon Durkheim anad Weber for especially important sociological direction. MacIver similarly specifies Weber and Mead as affording him crucial fundamental guidance. Sorokin likewise links himself with Comte's approach, along some elementary lines anyway. Each of those several European scientific sources contributed conspicuously toward sociology's emergence and distinction from other, related disciplines.[1] Each simultaneously exerted a corresponding influence fostering modern enlightenment's further development. It consequently should not be exactly surprising if we detect them evidencing the Kantian epistemological outlook quite strongly.

Parsons indicates the close relationship between Durkheim and Kant rather explicitly.[2] He does the same, albeit somewhat less directly, regarding the impact Kant had on Weber.[3] In a different context, though, he says Weber "was thoroughly steeped in Kantian thought."[4] Comte's compelling "French Connection'' made him a bit more impervious to the German idealist's complex theoretical constructions. He enthusiastically accepted, even extended, the scholarly autonomy concept however, and also the notion that empirical sense-data constituted the sole objectively given reality. His alleged ''Law of the Three Stages'' —religious, philosophical and positive (scientific)—obliquely accords with Kant's conception of philosophy's role, as replacing pure theology (interpreting Revelation), and preparing the way for scientific expansion.

Parsons leaves no doubt about his own faith in Kantian epistemology. One work affirms this belief twice. Very early there we are told: ''Whatever other philosophical position may be possible, I have explicitly taken one in the Kantian tradition. Starting with the objects of science in the strictest sense, this position maintains that the sense data that constitutes the empirical components of knowledge . . . must be articulated with the categories of understanding that are independent of the raw data.''[5] Again, near the end, we receive an additional explanation: ''Kant insisted that (against the empiricists . . . who stressed only sense impressions gained from outside the knower) there is another contribution from the categories of understanding (inside the knower) which has to be conceived as combining with sense data. The Kantian formula for empirical knowledge thus meets the formal requirements of a two-way relationship . . . between subject and object.''[6] He thus implicitly adopts the modern enlightened attitude—admitting only the sensible-empirical as ''really knowable''—and asserting humans' autonomous efforts at theoretically (subjectively) constructing, then practically (objectively) projecting, an empirically controlling order. Such a radically naturalistic (relatively romantic) outlook shows still more starkly through Parsons's systematic sociological output. Obviously we will consider the latter's explications here merely so far as they affect our overall theological interests.

Making certainty doubly sure on that supposedly scientific cognitive score, where it touches human affairs, Parsons inserts a confirmatory codicil: "We are dealing with the human condition from an anthropocentric point of view so that in this context we are giving symbolic meaning to the phenomena we are discussing. What we are not doing is to impute the apprehension and communication of meaning . . . to the objects that we are considering. We do not attempt to interpret what they are and do from their own 'subjective point of view,' as Weber called it."[7]

In other words, this sociologist (like his enlightened authorities) is utilizing the same interpretive approach that we previously saw employed by Einstein as a physicist.[8] Although the two areas so studied do display some similarities, drastic differences surely set them widely apart. Of course, if one accepts the Kantian epistemological dogma, there isn't very much objective basis for drawing sharp distinctions. Such a supremely simplistic or subtly subjectivistic cognitive stance may not pose severe conceptual dangers at the physical level, since the "substitious" or substitutional possibilities are less pronounced. When applied anthropologically, however, where profound biological and psychological factors combine, the subversive prospects become serious enough to start the "early warning" signals sounding. We need neither wait nor wonder long, either, before Parsons makes the suspected threat an expected reality.

An important "point of order" should be recognized and clarified first. It concerns our social scientist's rather basic referential concepts: action and interaction. These encompass human endeavors, he says: "In the relevant sense action is . . . specifically human, and concerns those aspects of human behavior which are involved in and controlled by culturally structured symbolic codes. . . . 'Acts' in this sense are behaviors to which their authors and those who significantly interact with them attribute . . . a 'subjective,' which is to say cultural or symbolic, meaning."[9]

Here we see Kant's subjective ''constructionist'' influence at work. The interacting agents impose meaning upon their mutual sensible contacts. That meaning carries a commonly accepted or conventional (cultural) content fundamentally, hence reflects a relatively contrived ''objectivity'' elementally. Those who thus knowingly use it (principally professionals) consequently are automatically, if subconsciously, inclined to stress self-made interpretations (discreetly) of the central conceptions, while theoretically expanding, and even more, practically extending them. The romantically enlightened, radically autonomous attitude only achieves its complete expression this way.

Parsons begins explaining human interaction with some psychological conceptualizations that he admits acquiring from Freud. Accordingly,

> two interacting persons must be conceived to be objects to each other in two primary respects and in a third respect which is in a sense derived from the first two. These are (1) cognitive perception and conceptualization, the answer to the question of what the object is, and (2) cathexis—attachment or aversion—the answer to the question of what the object means in an emotional sense. The third mode by which a person orients himself to an object is by evaluation—the integration of the cognitive and cathetic meanings of the object to form a system.[10]

In another place we find him saying such a distinction between cognition and cathexis was ''classically formulated for modern culture by Freud.''[11] Since Freud emphasized humans' sensible-material or biological aspects extravagantly, we may safely assume Parsons will do the same. That assumption is further supported by the latter's additional professional affection for Piaget; whose similar ''substitious'' (substitutional) predilections were observed earlier.[12] Sure enough, our not so great expectations are realized.

His later study on social systems and action theory identifies the cognitive and cathetic components as ''intelligence'' and ''affect'' respectively. He conceives the first to be ''a medium for circulation,'' like money: ''We treat it as a fluid resource which can be acquired . . . and effectively used by being 'spent'.''[13] Being merely a functional characteristic, ''trait'' or ''medium'' (instrumental), although one that constitutes the ''personality'' (cognitive competence), he sees it ''anchored in the behavioral system.''[14] This coincides closely with Piaget's dictum regarding the organic continuity between intelligence and sensori-motor or biological forces. ''Affect'' receives a rather complex classification—''another medium . . . conceived to circulate,'' but ''anchored in the social system.''[15] Parsons stresses ''affect's'' social connection because it holds so much importance for collective solidarity. ''Affect . . . is the generalized medium most definitely concerned with the mobilization and control of the factors of solidarity.'' Now ''moral order . . . is a primary regulator of solidary relationships,'' we are told.[16] Then comes the reason why affect must be mainly social: ''Affective attachment of individuals to the collectivities which are constitutive of the structure of the social system and to the other individuals who share membership status with them are at the center of the mechanisms by which general (human) action factors can achieve the status of institutionalization in defining the structure of social units.''[17]

Here we evidently have another notable example of Kant's rationalizing influence. Recall how the latter postulated God's existence, and humans' dependence upon Him, to stabilize their strictly rationally conceived moral order. Only if such is the case would individuals find sufficient motivation inclining them toward moral action. Parsons postulates ''affect's'' analogous grounding in the social system as the key factor insuring group loyalty or responsibility. That a priori ''objective'' assumption, strengthening a posteriori subjective conceptions concerning obligations, thus supposedly counters excessive individual tendencies.[18]

Nevertheless, since he adopts Piaget's view regarding intelligence's biological base, a similar cognitive correlation apparently applies when interpreting "affect's" proximate locus, within the human subject.[19] On this additional psychological score, Piaget tells us, "What common-sense calls 'feelings' and 'intelligence,' regarding them as two opposed 'faculties,' are simply behavior relating to persons and behavior affecting ideas or things; but in each of these forms of behavior, the same affective and cognitive aspects of action emerge, aspects which are in fact always associated and in no way represent independent faculties."[20]

Parsons accordingly demonstrates a decidedly "substitious" or substitutional conception of humans' essential content. Sensible-material or corporeal features definitely dominate their constitutional core. Through his modernistic scientific analysis, humanity's chief personal characteristics (thinking and expressing) become appraised as little more than higher and deeper emanations from the biological organism. Faithfully following his like-enlightened sociological and psychological mentors (Durkheim and Piaget), he denies—indirectly at least, any substantial-spiritual powers' pertinence. Consequent upon that largely fundamentalistic, quantitively slanted, behavioristic approach, functionalism serves as the principal analytical component. Form or structure, and end or purpose are merely ancillary aids facilitating overt action.[21] Such an activistic attitude aptly reflects his Kantian romantically rationalistic, naturalistic, theoretically secularistic heritage. It therefore correspondingly marks the general societal edifice that he constructs.

Considering the human person more comprehensively, as situated amid society's complexity, Parsons promptly reduces what he terms the "irreducibility of the distinctiveness of all human personalities" to a set of common categories.[22] These are subjectively contrived conceptions, certainly, yet allegedly represent objectively relevant "action" relationships inherent in all humans. He labels them "personality," "culture," and "organism."[23] Little or nothing is said about their content (what they are). Instead, he typically concentrates upon their portent (how they are); simply stamping those general attributes "subsystems of action," thus indicating their mainly functional significance. The said factors mutually interact: immediately or subjectively (inside the individual), and mediately or objectively (between individuals and groups). On the second count, Parsons classifies them as "environments" of the social system—itself another action-subsystem.

The "personality" apparently constitutes the individual's cognitive and emotive center—where intelligence and "affect" function. "Organism" obviously comprises the behavioral or biological system; while "culture" reflects the subjectively assimilated values, norms, and similar symbolic constructs chiefly derived from the overall societal "environments." Somehow these distinct but complementary "systems" consolidate, and so produce the individual human being. In the resulting vital dynamism that activates the latter, "personality" evidently is functionally concerned with ends or goals; "culture" inclined toward means; and "organism" geared to methods.[24] Parsons again affirms the bodily organism's critical "anchoring" contribution: as the base and seeming source for the various functions.[25]

This individual "action system," multiplied and unified, represents the societal system, Parsons says, implicitly anyway. Quite consistently, he makes the link between the "social system" and its members another functional factor. Neither the individual nor the "personality" (his counterpart-concept here) but a "role," enacted by the participant, provides the fundamental unifying force. "Role" involves a definite action-status or responsibility that one exercises among a society's membership. The same subject ordinarily fills several "roles," in different divisions of the "social system."[26] Collective solidarity requires adapting individuals' interests and needs regarding their vital constituents ("personality," "culture," and "organism") to similar common concerns. These then become the "environments" with which the "social system's" collectivities interpenetrate, and by which they are functionally distinguished.[27]

21

Parsons sees the principal collective units (''subsystems'') forming the ''social system'' as political, cultural (including religious, educational, scientific, and artistic agencies), familial, and economic. Each impinges especially upon a specific ''environment.'' Through such systematic 'interpenetrations,'' each collectivity promotes proportionate advances for the members' pertinent dynamic sector. Thus, the political ''subsystem'' fosters the ''personality environment's'' functional orientation toward ends or ''goal attainment.'' The cultural ''subsystem'' facilitates the ''cultural environment's'' efforts at developing the values and norms (means) insuring stable and integral functional progress (''pattern maintenance''). The family supplies a closely related stabilizing societal service, but along somewhat less concentrated lines. Most prominently, economic collectivities (a conceptualistic, not a Communistic, term) enhance the organism-environment's functional dependence on better ways and technical means of exploiting surrounding physical and biological resources.[28]

Parsons's preferential testimony to function's vital predominance over structure and purpose necessarily follows from his sense-confined notions regarding objective reality. With only sensible empirical data acceptable, he cannot allow more than marginal (corporeal) substantive content in human relations, rationally considered at least. Their vaunted ''constructionist'' or conceptually projectionistic abilities are interpreted largely as a built-in ''cybernetics system,'' spawned by the biological organism's ''genetic code.''[29] Lacking any significant objective spiritual-substantial insights concerning ''personality'' (although the entire cognitive-affective process actually affords them), such a ''substitious'' (substitutional) scientist naturally exhibits the same deficiency toward reality as a whole. Admitting religion's relevant supernatural social ramifications, Parsons says ''there must be something there in the sense of a potential cognitively understandable set of objects.''[30] Because these cannot be contacted through the bodily organism, however, they merely may be subjectively conceived and represented.

"Sensible-minded," body-bounded people like Parsons never "get off the ground," except theoretically, socially speaking. Hard-core believers in epistemological self-projections, especially on the psychological plane, they derive a pseudospiritual lift from the plausibility accorded them by self-believing fellow professionals, and perhaps similarly self-indulgent ordinary followers.

ADDITIONAL SOCIOLOGICAL ENLIGHTENMENT

1. We previously noted Sorokin's affirmation of his adherence to Comte's sociological viewpoint in certain central respects; and also the latter's less concentrated Kantian connections, compared with other early sociologists (Durkheim and Weber). Whether those limited relationships affected the stance or not, the former apparently basically rejects both the enlightened empiricists' and constructionists' sensibly founded faith. He believes the human mind can penetrate reality's content objectively, beyond the initially given sense-data. As he explains this natural facility,

> One of the highest forms of combining activity of the mind is its abstracting function. It consists in an ability to observe and abstract similarity, uniformity, and connection among apparent disparities and perceptual dissimilarities of phenomena. This mode of combination is not confined to perceptional similarity, contiguity or contrast. It goes beyond such combinations and gives us, in its mature form, the causal connections of phenomena, causal uniformity, and the typical in the arts and sciences . . . or adequate definition.[31]

The conceptions thus derived, not contrived, are not alone adequate for human knowledge, but must be additionally checked and correlated, sensibly and rationally. He therefore advises us, "This does not mean . . . that intuition alone is sufficient . . . the initial enlightenment it supplies must be checked, tested, and developed by logic or reason, and by empirical sensory observation . . . intuition serves as the foundation of the validity of the basic propositions . . . of religion, ethics, philosophy, aesthetics . . . and scientific thought."[32]

When applying that fundamental epistemological position scientifically though (psychologically and sociologically), Sorokin adopts a mainly "substitious" or substitutional approach, rather resembling Parsons.

Sorokin acknowledges an existentially recognizable human "superempirical or transcendental (spiritual) soul." He further sees, "this super-conscious 'egoless soul' . . . (as the) ultimate agent integrating our biological and conscious egos into unity."[33] Nevertheless, much like Parsons's (and Kant's) enlightened exclusion by exaltation, such a core vital principle has no scientific significance, we learn. He banishes it with the simplistic statement, "its analysis belongs to religion and metaphysics." At the psychological level, then, the person becomes a prey to fragmenting tendencies, which Sorokin plainly approves: "My thesis is that the individual has not one empirical soul, or self, or ego, but several: first, biological, and second, social egos. The individual has as many different social egos as there are different social groups and strata with which he is connected. These egos are as different from one another as the social groups and strata from which they spring."[34]

This largely quantitive or sharply sensible empirical attitude really reflects Parsons's functionalism—where the individual appears as a "bundle" of "action"—involvements. Structure merely serves as a convenient conceptual "string," one could correctly say, to tie the collection together theoretically, and make it ultimately unified. Under that highly artificial arrangement organic or biological factors necessarily enjoy a decided advantage over their spiritual vital counterparts. Caught between those contrary ego pressures, and lacking more than a fundamental central control, a person can hardly be sure about what he or she is doing, especially on critical occasions. Sorokin poses the serious problem at issue here, and calmly leaves it "hanging in the air." After remarking how "an individual's culture depends upon his selectivity and creativity," he casually admits there may be conflicting notions concerning the cause: "Whether their selection and creativity depend upon biological constitution or upon something much more subtle and intangible which we can designate as transcendental soul . . . this problem remains open."[35]

Purpose receives a somewhat similar subsidiary interpretation, being considered pertinent only when fully consciously or explicitly stimulating action.[36] Its continuing implicit coordinating dynamic contributions are denied, consequently allowing greater scope for biological mechanisms.

On the societal score too, the connection with Parsons shows quite clearly. Not the individuals themselves but their social "egos" or roles constitute the basic social units.[37] The functional vector accordingly becomes the chief dynamic component here also. Instead of stressing substantive stability, then, even amid evolutionary process, the tangible and variable gets prime attention. Like Parsons, Sorokin rather views the former ("egos") mainly as theoretical categories (although representing reality elementally), while affording the latter (function) practical emphasis. Thus, harmony between a person's social egos is said to stem solely from harmony among his or her related groups.[38] One's "transcendental soul" supplies no significant integrating help, it seems, except perhaps through the blind (conveniently subjectively contrived) belief, which Kant advocated. So identifying personal peace with social solidarity certainly places a premium upon human life's external or corporeal content.

Sorokin's principal "social systems" or collectivities closely match those that Parsons conceives. He distinguishes political, cultural (religious, educational, etc.), familial, and economic.[39] If his observations in these respects manifest more specialized refinements, they lack at least one important generalized correlation. They do not directly link the societal units and humans' fundamental vital dynamism—ends, means, methods, as Parsons's do. Despite Sorokin's acceptance of a supernatural reality, its sociological impact is scarcely more relevant for him than for Parsons. From his romantic, scientifically earthbound standpoint, this "superempirical" sphere represents a radical antithesis to the natural order. It therefore parallels societally the "superconscious," "egoless" soul's personal role. Both are carefully "cordoned off," being permitted merely a remote influence on the sensible-empirical. Each may serve as ultimate consolational, even inspirational sources, but not proximate assisting forces, when struggling at maintaining balance between competing egos, individually and socially.[40]

2. Although assertedly adopting Weber's sociological approach (earlier termed strongly Kantian by Parsons), MacIver evidently escapes the former's categorically projectionistic attitude. Like Sorokin, he too believes the human mind can penetrate reality objectively, beyond the sensibly empirical.[41] Still, because he also reflects modern scientists' romantically enlightened autonomy (emulating Kant there at least); his ensuing interpretations of the human situation bear the sharply sensibly slanted stamp. Resembling Weber, then, and the other original mentor mentioned before, Mead, MacIver displays a definite "substitious" or substitutional bent. That compromised characteristic can be discerned in the concentrated attention focused upon his topics' tangible quantitive features, compared with the relatively loose and lateral sort shown their intangible qualitive aspects.

He defines human individuality, for example, "in the sociological sense," as "that attribute which reveals the member of a group as . . . a self, a center of activity and response expressive of a nature that is his own."[42]

This definition certainly could cover any organic species' members, subject to differences of degree, qualitatively and quantitatively. Only if humans possess a superorganic vital capacity—discriminating freedom—can one correctly classify them as significantly or radically different (in kind) from other "selves" and "centers of activity." Yet MacIver does not accept such a superior, really spiritual (temporally and spacially surmounting) view regarding humanity.[43] Furthermore, he simply contrasts human "individuality" "in the sociological sense" alongside physical and biological "individuality." At another place, however, he says, "society is not limited to human beings. There are animal societies of many degrees."[44] His sociological distinction consequently remains principally within the biological sphere.

The tangible quantitive factor receives even greater emphasis, again implicitly, where he distinguishes "personality" as a human component: "Personality . . . is all that an individual is and has experienced so far as this 'all' can be comprehended as a unity. Personality is thus a much broader term than individuality, for personality embraces the total 'organized aggregate of psychological processes and states pertaining to the individual.' "[45]

"Personality" accordingly represents the "self's" range or quantity of psychical constitutents. Since these are simply said to be "organized" (organic), and individual "processes" or "states," the overall or total condition equivalently reflects humans' higher biological hence sociological development. MacIver's excessively sensible-empirical attitude toward morals rather confirms the foregoing estimates concerning his "substitious" or substitutional inclinations. Actually surpassing Parsons's stress on functionalism here, the former equates morals and mores.[46] They consequently can and should change, like any collectively contrived value or norm, consonant with popularly plausible preferences.

MacIver classifies the principal social groupings (he labels them associations) along the same lines as Parsons and Sorokin.[47] One somewhat notable variation includes the familial among the cultural divisions, although Parsons did indicate their close connection. Resembling Sorokin, he does not directly correlate the said associations and humans' basic dynamic processes—ends, means, and methods. All three do agree, however, in interpreting the political societal unit as the prime authority for determining, and promoting, a complete community's (national, regional, local) purposes or goals. Despite the fact that they admit those ends are founded upon moral values and norms, besides the latter being derived mainly from religious sources, the polity is considered the social agency that chiefly controls effective action here. While the three similarly acknowledge the Church's religious and moral institutional role, its disunity, but still more its claim of "super-empirical" authority, inclines them toward limiting its social import to the private cultural realm. By so circumscribing this entity's social contribution, and correspondingly enhancing the political ones, these enlightened sociologists further exemplify their conviction regarding the tangible temporal or sensible empirical order's superior vital significance. Actually, then, all are Kantian, romantic "Knowers," scientifically or sociologically.

MacIver surely displays such a mentality succinctly, when he says, "Science discovers the external forms and forces of the cosmos. . . . Science is not only the explorer of the nature of things but also its interpreter. . . . The vision thus attainable and the conception of the infinite power that holds atoms and galaxies and everything between in their appointed ways are the preconditions of any religion worthy of modern man."[48]

3. Along with the three rather eminent sociologists thus summarily surveyed, another, quite different (as almost religiously reverent), one deserves attention. He is Peter Berger, a contemporary social scientist who doubles at "dealing" (if not dabbling) in theology. His principal professional competence concerns the "sociology of knowledge." His name and fame, however, probably have been built upon extensive efforts at making the supernatural socially respectable, if not entirely acceptable, today. The latter labor has made him currently popular among many religious-minded academicians, though perhaps not so many theologians. Combining a fundamentalistic, faintly angel-

ical (even evangelical) religious interest, and a very pragmatic, pointedly heretical emphasis, this tangential theological enterprise carries a certain easygoing conviction. By subtly blending an elemental traditional touch with the romantically enlightened modernistic trait, this sophisticated sociological entrepreneur evidently expects to provide a prominently plausible and proportionately marketable religious product.

Berger's major strictly sociological study outlines a "sociology of knowledge." It also reveals the sources of his scientific faith. Its title, *The Social Construction of Reality,* immediately marks him as a Kantian believer.[49] Translating such a categorically contrived, projectionistic viewpoint regarding reality into sociological terms, we get collective constructionistic results. The work identifies relatively explicit Kantian witnesses—Durkheim and Weber, and rather implicit ones—Marx and Mead, as the author's proximate mentors. Berger accordingly aims at maintaining modern sociological orthodoxy. Theoretically focussing on society's understandable content does not represent any departure from his colleagues' "enlightened" scientific stand either. Those early sociologists likewise manifested much interest in religion's import for culture, as subsequent social scholars have done too, if less extensively. Berger's decidedly distinctive sociological significance rests upon the prominence he affords religion's supernatural element. Not surprisingly, though, he adopts and advocates that crypto-theological approach while simultaneously insuring fidelity to the modern scientific attitude. Given the latter's solely sensibly supported (subjectively and objectively) theoretical contrivances (constructionistic interpretations), the ensuing extravagant effort literally resembles a corporeal "bootstrap"-lifting, or a biblical "Babel"-building operation.

Consistent with his bodily bound basic beliefs concerning the really "knowable" (dogma derived from Kant's followers), Berger sees the human subject mainly as a biological organism.[50] He doesn't bother about finer analytical distinctions along lines drawn by Parsons, Sorokin, and MacIver here. This comparatively lessens his dissembling effect somewhat. Otherwise they approximately agree. The said self-conscious unit cannot promote its own integrity and stability autonomously; hence inherently inclines toward social relations.[51] Through such interaction, and resulting socialization, each individual develops a "higher self."[52] That enhanced (as enlarged) existence entails more than mere "biological data."[53] It includes subjectively contrived conceptions interpreting the same, and projected thereon, thus constructing a meaningful societal system. The "knowledge" or culture so devised and applied constitutes the objective collective order, and the subjective, individually reflected counterpart thereof; both being decisively sensibly conditioned.[54] Since the fundamental foundation and framework for these relationships are material (biological and physical), the entire pronouncedly quantitive dynamic process ceaselessly, practically completely changes. Like the other modernistically enlightened social scientists, therefore, Berger finds the historical (viewed empirically in temporal and spatial terms) chiefly controlling social and individual development.[55]

Berger believes this thoroughgoing relativizing impact of history helps rather than hampers "knowledge." His later study on the supernatural says: "Once we know all human affirmations are subject to scientifically graspable socio-historical processes, which affirmations are true and which false?. . . . What follows . . . is a new freedom and flexibility in asking questions of truth."[56]

Even theologians supposedly benefit from such a relativistic theoretical attitude, according to him. It sets them "free of dogmatic opinions." He consequently suggests they start with the assumption that, "in, with, and under the immense array of human projections, there are indicators of a reality that is truly other."[57] He further believes anthropology will provide the best link between theology and the said scientific outlook. "This new awareness . . . tends toward inductive modes of theological thought,'' we are told. The latter approach affords the most encouraging prospects regarding efforts at rekindling a largely lost interest in the supernatural, Berger asserts. ''It is the method of 'inductive faith' that holds the greatest promise of a new approach to religious truth in the intellectual situation marked by a pervasive sense of relativity,'' we learn.[58]

Berger's exorbitant emphasis upon ''inductive faith,'' echoing his earlier noted colleagues' functionalism, especially exemplifies the practical penalty paid for their grand illusion or fantasized faith—identifying objectively ''knowable'' empirical reality as strictly sensible (''fallacy of misplaced concreteness''). Pathetically confused by such a ''substitious'' or substitutional stand, these so epistemologically subverted believers see inductive or synthetic reason producing faith. Actually, though, the causal relationship is the other way around, basically. No amount of factual data, howsoever numerous and voluminous, can be truly systematically integrated, unless the observer has certain guiding assumptions (values and norms). Those initial conceptions concerning the things' ultimate meaning (causal connections) are the dogmas with which all thinkers (even scientists) must start. Through subsequent experimental observation and reasonable reflection, the investigator will arrive at additional more or less general conclusions always formulated within the framework that their fundamental postulate allows. They thus really represent projections (extensions) from the basic belief, or distinct, yet still originally dependent, developments in understanding. The so inductively derived insights accordingly actualize the initial faith's covert implications, thereby possibly confirming and strengthening, but not producing it. Obviously, a complementary deductive process is similarly involved.

Berger implicitly testifies to the foregoing facts regarding faith, saying: ''Faith, in the proper meaning of the word, is or is not held . . . no learning is necessary.''[59] Faith antecedes learning at all levels—on the primordial ("world-view") plane, and the succeeding subsidiary commitments activating it, theoretically and practically. "What kind of faith?" constitutes the crucially relevant question. Ultimately, hence morally, this demands one's distinguishing between natural and supernatural faith: the first chiefly external, sensible-material, physically and biologically bound; the second mainly internal, intellectual-spiritual, metaphysically loosed. Admittedly, either view's acceptance requires preliminary factual or empirical evidence, including personal example, as support. Humans' corporeal connections necessitate their synthesizing diverse perceptions to facilitate formulating general conceptions. For faith, however, such synthetic effort does not comprise an inductive reasoning exercise (although an overall causal linkage implicitly occurs). Rather does it entail a concerted summary perception, and a corresponding conceptual insight—an integral intuition (wisdom). Some lateral learning—experiential (circumstantial combinations) and rational (cognitive correlations)—precedes the fundamental faith act therefore. Nevertheless, the more thoroughly relevant, consolidating and completing (inductive and deductive) learning (knowledge and discovery) follows from faith's inception and application. The etymology of the term "epistemology" emphasizes that fact—Greek *epistis* meaning from the source, or postulate, dogma, belief.[60]

All faith or belief, then, especially ultimate faith, is a gift basically, founded upon evidence supplied by empirical reality's source (revelation). Is this source merely superficially "other," as essentially sensible-material-external, "topped off" with humans' higher biological conceptive and projective ("constructionist") powers? Or is it truly supernaturally "other," as essentially intelligible-spiritual-internal, with human intelligence and volitional freedom (properly responsibly employed) remotely reflecting a divine personal Power? We must make a critical, vitally determining choice. Berger equates the latter and heresy, due to the original Greek connection—*hairesis,* meaning choice. He has written a book on that choice theme, avidly explaining how a person must be a heretic to be free.[61]

It represents a typical, modernistically enlightened, professional "magical" feat—replete with "mirrors," refracting his naturalistic-secularistic, sensible-empirical, subjectively centered standard for choice as the sole valid one. Those who choose the opposite, more objective, supernatural-religious alternative, acknowledging a suprasensible empirical content, and attendant inherent spiritual values and norms insuring morally responsible secular constructions and projections, are allegedly the prey of fate.

Since he confronts the epistemological problem rather directly, measured against the other sociologists' positions considered previously, somewhat like Harvey and Kant (their major mentor), Berger better illustrates the fate to which such self-enlightened scientists have committed themselves. By envisioning empirical reality strictly in their own autonomously conceived or believed image, they cannot consciously contact the supernatural realm. They cannot see ("discover") its manifestation "in, with, and under the immense array of human projections," because they do not really believe that is possible, despite declared good intentions. Bound interiorly through a dogmatic bent toward an exterior, sensible revelation alone, whatever they see symbolically must be interpreted naturalistically, or mainly materially. Accepting only this evidence objectively, one has no available cognitive means allowing a spiritual or supernatural "breakthrough."

Lacking a fundamental faith-conversion, then, Berger and his "substitious" fellow scientists have but two viable alternatives regarding their supernatural suspicions. Either believe blindly, as a conveniently devised and desired theoretical projection, thereby supposedly protecting both their practical "supernaturalism" and secularism—like Kant and "Company." Or be honest, and persist in their secularistic "constructionist" pursuits, as the popularly and professionally preferred, plausible attitude; ignoring inveterately any supernatural possibilities. No person, not even autonomously enlightened modernists, can serve two masters, ultimately, that is.

NOTES

1. T. Raison, ed., *The Founding Fathers of Social Science* (London: Scholar Press, 1979).

2. Parsons, *Social Systems,* pp. 160–162.

3. Ibid., pp. 162–163.

4. From *Action Theory and the Human Condition* by Talcott Parsons. Copyright © 1978 by the Free Press, a division of Macmillan, Inc., p. 356.

5. From *Action Theory and the Human Condition* by Talcott Parsons. Copyright © 1978 by the Free Press, a division of Macmillan, Inc., p. 5.

6. From *Action Theory and the Human Condition* by Talcott Parsons. Copyright © 1978 by the Free Press, a division of Macmillan, Inc., p. 368.

7. From *Action Theory and the Human Condition* by Talcott Parsons. Copyright © 1978 by the Free Press, a division of Macmillan, Inc., p. 372.

8. Einstein, "Physics and Reality."

9. From *Social Systems and the Evolution of Action Theory* by Talcott Parsons. Copyright © 1977 by the Free Press, a division of Macmillan, Inc., p. 230.

10. From *Social Structure and Personality* by Talcott Parsons. Copyright © 1964 by the Free Press, a division of Macmillan, Inc., pp. 20–21.

11. From *Action Theory and the Human Condition* by Talcott Parsons. Copyright © 1978 by the Free Press, a division of Macmillan, Inc., p. 369.

12. Piaget, *Intelligence,* p. 6–7.

13. From *Social Systems and the Evolution of Action Theory* by Talcott Parsons. Copyright © 1977 by the Free Press, a division of Macmillan, Inc., p. 216.

14. From *Social Structure and Personality* by Talcott Parsons. Copyright © 1964 by the Free Press, a division of Macmillan, Inc., p. 215.

15. From *Social Structure and Personality* by Talcott Parsons. Copyright © 1964 by the Free Press, a division of Macmillan, Inc., pp. 218–219.

16. From *Social Structure and Personality* by Talcott Parsons. Copyright © 1964 by the Free Press, a division of Macmillan, Inc., p. 219.

17. From *Social Structure and Personality* by Talcott Parsons. Copyright © 1964 by the Free Press, a division of Macmillan, Inc.

18. Ibid.

19. Kant naturally conceived morality as having a source in the human subject also. A person could not act responsibly otherwise. Parsons implies the same with "affect," saying the latter entails "commitments of individual persons to participation in solidary collectivities." It entails too, an "allocation . . . between the societal and nonsocietal commitments."—Ibid.

He further implies a biological foundation here: "The organism (behavioral) is also the source of the 'instinctual' components of the motivation of individuals' personalities."—Ibid., p. 192.

20. Piaget, *Intelligence*, p. 6.

21. Parsons, *Social Systems*, p. 236; Parsons, *Action Theory*, pp. 361–367.

22. Parsons, *Social System*, p. 197.

23. Ibid., pp. 191–198.

24. Ibid., cf. Parsons, *System of Modern Societies* (Englewood Cliffs: Prentice Hall, 1971), p. 6.

25. Parsons, *Social Systems*, p. 196.

26. Ibid., and pp. 163, 182.

27. Ibid., pp. 182–183, 202.

28. Ibid., pp. 192–196, 201, 254–255.

29. Ibid., pp. 234–236.

30. From *Action Theory and the Human Condition* by Talcott Parsons. Copyright © 1978 by the Free Press, a division of Macmillan, Inc., pp. 357, 370–371; Parsons, p. 194.

31. P. A. Sorokin, *Society, Culture, and Personality* (New York: Cooper Square Publishing, 1969), p. 560. Excerpts reprinted by permission of Rowman and Allanheld, Publishers.

32. Ibid., pp. 546–547.

33. Ibid., p. 345, note 11.

34. Ibid., p. 345.

35. Ibid., p. 356.

36. Ibid., pp. 44–47.

37. Ibid., pp. 39–41.

38. Ibid., pp. 351–355.

39. Ibid., chapters 11 and 12.

40. Ibid., chapters 41 and 42.

41. R. M. MacIver and C. H. Page, *Society, An Introductory Analysis* (New York: Holt, Rinehart & Winston, 1962), pp. 4–5. Excerpts reprinted by permission of Charles H. Page.

42. Ibid., p. 50.

43. Ibid., p. 51.

44. Ibid., pp. 6–7.

45. Ibid., p. 56.

46. Ibid., pp. 18–22; 197–199. "[Ethical] valuations [are] socially conditioned [and] subjective." Ibid., p. 529.

47. Ibid., chapters 11, 18, 19, 20.

48. Bramson, *On Society*, pp. 297–298.

49. Excerpt from *The Social Construction of Reality* by Peter Benger and Thomas Lockmann. Copyright © 1966 by Peter L. Berger and Thomas Luckmann. Reprinted by permission of Doubleday & Company, Inc.

50. Ibid., pp. 180–182.

51. Ibid., pp. 51–52.

52. Ibid., pp. 181–182.

53. Ibid., p. 52.

54. Ibid., pp. 92–128.

55. Ibid., Introduction.

56. Peter L. Berger, *A Rumor of Angels* (New York: Doubleday, 1969), pp. 50, 53. Excerpts from *A Rumor of Angels* by Peter Berger. Copyright © 1969 by Peter L. Berger. Reprinted by permission of Doubleday & Company, Inc.

57. Ibid., p. 60.

58. Ibid., p. 96.

59. Ibid., p. 97; Cf. Parkes, *Gods and Men*, p. 473; A. R. Gini, "William James: Facts, Faith and Promise," *The Thomist*, 37 (July, 1973): 499ff.

60. K. Rahner, *Foundations of Christian Faith*, W. V. Dych, trans. (New York: Seabury, 1978), pp. 8–10, 231.

61. Peter L. Berger, *The Heretical Imperative* (New York: Anchor/Doubleday), 1979.

Part II

Chapter Three

TRADITIONAL REALISTIC ENLIGHTENMENT

Through the foregoing observations, we have seen how the fatal fallacy characterizing modernistically enlightened, professional sociological thinkers involves adherence to a ''substitious'' or sensibly subverted epistemology (ideology). Admitting sense-data alone as objectively knowable, they immunize themselves from reality's substantive impact, consciously at least. Actually, of course, all the elegant theoretical interpretations they allegedly entirely construct manifest subconscious connections with those inner spiritual forces, subjectively and objectively. Such complex conceptual engagements never could be commenced, much less completed, if the so acting subjects, and the relevant objects, lacked correspondingly compatible and communicable content. Except for an obstinately arbitrary and acutely autonomous attitude, these subjectivistic social scientists have no more valid reasons justifying sense-data's reliability than the immaterial interior kind. Like their independent-minded predecessors and contemporaries, though, they prefer the former presumption (faith), since it seemingly insures the greatest personal autonomy, and proportionate professional plausibility. Humanity, then, is viewed either in strictly secular, mainly material terms (howsoever high), or as approximating divinity practically (''religiously'' following

Luther and Kant).[1] Both beliefs represent what could correctly be called a "shrinkers" outlook; the first belittling man, the second blaspheming God (hence more reprehensible). Both thus reflect a shirking of human humility and realistic responsibility.

Mortimer Adler affords us an instructive historical summary regarding the basic error that marks and so mars Kant's epistemology. "Of all the little errors in the beginning that have plagued modern philosophy since its start," he says, "the most serious is the one that was made in the psychology of cognition."[2] The error began with Descartes, we are told. It was adopted by Locke, and passed along via Hume to Kant. The mistake entailed two false notions, Adler explains: "The first is the error of regarding ideas as the objects that we directly apprehend when we are conscious. . . . The second is the error of failing to distinguish between sense and intellect as cognitive powers which, while they are cooperative in the cognitive process, do not operate in the same way and do not contribute in the same way to whatever knowledge we are able to achieve."[3]

Rather than confronting those new theories directly, he adds, Kant "tried to circumvent them with an ingeniously confected theory of mind." Such a radically independent approach exemplifies the latter's exuberant romantic emphasis upon "enlightenment" that we noted earlier. It especially stressed the logical or theoretical construction of "objects": things not apprehended in themselves (inner reality), but only in their external sensible features, as also observed above. From this false start, modern thought still suffers: "Post-Kantian thought, both in the 19th and 20th centuries, is not only a record of diverse reactions to Kant's inventions but also a record of self-defeating attempts to solve problems that would not be problems at all if the errors initially made . . . had been corrected."[4]

"The only way out of the debacle of modern philosophy," Adler concludes, "is to go back to its beginning and try to make a fresh start." The problem clearly concerns sociology too, as

40

we have seen previously. Before following his advice, however, it appears appropriate to consider the probable personal motivation behind Kant's monumental misconceptions.

Our preceding investigations have shown how Kant was profoundly influenced by the secular scientific outlook gradually gaining momentum after Luther's religious revolt, and the ensuing radical divorce between the natural and supernatural realms. They likewise indicated his leading role in the modern enlightenment's effort at establishing human autonomy on a near absolute scale. He consistently advocated reason's ultimate importance, as the crucial factor controlling personal development. While ostensibly admitting the need for a supernatural relationship, he conceived this mainly along supplementary, supporting lines. It supposedly served to confirm, even guarantee, humans' largely independent rational endeavors. Although God's existence is beyond reasonable demonstration from Kant's viewpoint, it was postulated by him out of practical necessity. Only with that contrived supernatural assistance could his naturally devised moral system be effectively employed. The basic dogma underlying such an epistemological and ethical system demands belief in humanity's radical rational, hence moral, autonomy; an arbitrarily decided and declared self-assertion.

What more logically completing conceptual framework might one erect upon this foundational faith (ideology), insuring its overt implementation, than the kind that an additional dogma, concerning reality's subjective constructionist meaning, allows?[5] Human thought thus virtually assumes an ultimately definitive dynamic role regarding the subjects' destinies. The latter, then, are allegedly free to establish their own values and norms, through presumed inherent interpretative powers. At the same time, a person may, if so disposed, accept these theoretical determinations as reflecting God's will; because of his or her fundamentalistic belief that God graciously approves humans' autonomous activity.

The traditional epistemological theory prevailing in the Western world, from the late Middle Ages to the time of Descartes, is known as "representational realism."[6] This title indicates its thoroughly positive attitude toward objectively given reality, envisioning the existing empirical order as both substantially and sensibly understandable, and assuming the human subject's corresponding (spiritual and corporeal) cognitive ability. Here we have the humbler approach: with mankind mainly measured by, rather than measuring, a magnified whole, consequently permitting growth beyond their own subjectively constructed and constricted conceptions. Such a profoundly bold belief sees the human mind passing through things' sensible features and grasping the inner constituent elements, Adler states. The former does not simply devise or discern ideas, indirectly depicting the entities under consideration, but actually attains their objectively intelligible content. Those penetrating insights' resulting representations, though obviously less than the things as concrete wholes, nevertheless contain real reflections of some substantial aspect. The knower thus becomes intensively or interiorly related to the latter mentally.[7]

From these inherent capacities for conceiving more or less objectively inclusive and subjectively exclusive, or temporally and spatially transcendent, actualities and potentialities in empirical reality; and for correlating them proportionately by reflective evaluating judgments; thereafter freely overtly expressing them via aptly constructed and selected material instruments, we recognize humans' personal or immanent (self-controlling), spiritual powers.[8] Similarly, through the so discovered intelligible order permeating the physical-biological types comprising humans' existential environment, we recognize the presence of impersonal, chiefly extrinsically influenced, substantiating spiritual powers. Both angelic and human agents exercise a crucial control over them. The empirically given is not solely sensible-material therefore, but likewise intelligible-spiritual.[9]

The concept provides the critically important contribution to the understanding process. As on the entitive plane, so at the cognitive level, conception starts the vital dynamism. In the traditional epistemological interpretation, cognition begins with some thing making an impact upon a subject's external sensible organ(s). The ensuing impression or percept becomes transferred to the imagination as an immaterial phantasm. From that particular stimulus, the mind's spiritual faculty or intellect abstracts or apprehends its universal, essential content (intelligible species), simultaneously identifying this as characterizing the concrete stimulating thing. Such is the concept: containing, then, not the latter as actually existing in itself, rather obtaining its objective communicable reflection.[10]

A real mental union accordingly occurs between the entity thus conceived and the apprehending person. The said conscious relationship entails more than an awareness of the known's segregated quality on the knower's part too. It further includes spontaneously reconnecting the intelligible species and the sensible phantasm, concomitantly noting the so mentally grasped essential quality's existence in the thing observed. The concept consequently carries, automatically, an objectively activated apprehension, and an accompanying, similarly sparked insight (implicit judgment) regarding its representation's existential import. Reality's objective, categorical aspects are not initially and fundamentally constructed and projected by the understanding person, therefore. They are rightly recognized as received (intuited) instead; constituting given, guiding, basically meaningful truths, or components of truth at least. With their clearer elucidation and closer comparative correlation, through additional experience and reasoned reflection thereon (judgment explicitly), constructions and projections are properly applied to the potentialities or capacities thus conceived, as more or less inherent therein.[11] That comprises realistic cognitive development.

The aforesaid underlying, unifying conceptions concerning

the thing sensibly perceived obviously do not depict its entire essential content. They merely focus upon certain central characteristics. From this simple start, however, the so mentally alerted agent is further activated toward achieving additional, like-linked (intuitive-judgmental) apprehensions of the objectively given entity, directly and indirectly. Besides discerning other elemental features in such thing, and between things, the mind's innate distinguishing ability simultaneously prompts the person's own self-identification on a comparative intelligible scale. Humans' typical reasoning power (formal judgment) becomes increasingly involved, reflectively combining and contrasting relations, thus gradually erecting the knowledgeable edifice. Aided by an ever-expanding historical or existential experience—sensible-corporeal (largely quantitive) and spiritual-substantial (mainly qualitive), these free agents have the cognitive capacity for an endlessly growing, understanding endeavor, chiefly through their temporally and spatially transcending conceptual and judgmental resources. The latter always mingle with corresponding contemporary corporeal connections or perceptions, though, so long as the process entails tangible entities. That developing dynamism's inner and outer aspects evidence a concerted evolutionary exigency, decisively self-determined in its overall outcome; yet under the recognizable limitations (personal) and obligations (communal) which flow from human beings' essential and existential dependency. Those impressional mental (intellectual-imaginative-sensitive) faculties naturally are influenced proportionately (rightly or wrongly) by complementary emotional expressional (volitional-vegetative-sensitive) powers.[12]

Such a realistic cognitional process works both synthetically and analytically, or inductively and deductively, on a mutually corroborating, even concomitantly completing, scale. The physical-biological sciences, the more technical human sciences and arts—politics, economics, domestic, history, medicine, physical-cultural anthropology—inevitably incline toward an inductive-synthetic, theoretical approach. Nevertheless, they likewise must employ the alternate one, if only subconsciously, as a necessary integrating support. Contrarily, the relatively more profound, proximately or directly substantive human sciences and arts—psychology, sociology, philosophical anthropology, philosophy, fine arts—properly emphasize the deductive-analytic, theoretical attitude. They must take the opposite understanding tack too, continually, as a needed counterbalancing, diversifying source.[13]

The mental disciplines or areas of cognition thus distinguishable represent humans' systematized judgments interpreting their experience with reality, as regards themselves and other contingent types, objectively and subjectively considered. Those cultural accumulations accordingly contain logically arranged (generically and specifically) conceptualizations that reflect, more or less accurately, the essential meanings (causal relationships) characterizing existing entities; as manifesting their intelligible or objectively given content. They also include, to a greater or lesser degree (directly or indirectly), the subjective, individuating features that largely materially (but spiritually too) mark each extant agent existentially. On the whole, then, human understanding mainly discloses reality's concretely situated, constitutive natures; derived from empirically founded, conceptual-judgmental-expressional, or reflective-responsive, experience. It always is incomplete, though, requiring continuing improvement, because of reality's infinite essential and existential richness.[14]

Looking back, momentarily, at the foregoing distinctions between the inductive-synthetic and deductive-analytic understanding procedures, we recall how the former concentrates principally upon the tangible, corporeal, rather quantitive factors in the things (subjects-objects) observed. The latter reverses the process, stressing instead the studied thing's intangible, immanently substantial-spiritual, qualitive aspects. Both strategies are seen as intrinsically interpenetrating and overlapping. This theoretical systematizing dialectic actually depicts, while enormously expanding along increasingly sophisticated lines, the fundamental human noetic effort. That initial mental endeavor was found to combine an external sensible impression—converted as an imaginal phantasm, and an intellectual abstraction therefrom, thus forming an existentially based, objectively derived, implicitly judgmental concept. The thing so apprehended is known in its simplest or most extreme outlines: something is; or its barest supplemental-sensible, existential, and its starkest elemental-intelligible, essential components. The existential and the sensible are originally identified on account of their readily evident similarity: entailing a quantitive (prominently particular) conglomerate. Whereas essential items, being profoundly qualitive (generic and specific), hence really semitranscendent or multirepresentable, have merely an indirectly and reflectively (not a spontaneously) recognizable existence.[15]

Additional experience with empirically available agents, accompanied by relevant reflection, generates sharper delineated as well as differentiated judgmental concepts; and the distinctively dynamic formal judgments correlating them. The resulting understanding consequently chiefly exhibits extensive elucidations of the essential qualities inherently characterizing the innumerable interrelated things (subjects-objects) existentially confronted. When embracing lower level abstractions and large-scale sensible data (like the physical-biological orders), understanding is primarily (not solely) inductive-synthetic. On the higher abstracting planes (uniquely human order), carrying progressively less detailed sensible connections, it especially (not entirely) exemplifies the deductive-analytic course.[16]

Beyond the aforesaid generic and specific essential distinctions, discerned as comprising qualitative-substantial unifying capacities, controlling integrally related quantitative-supplemental, diversifying traits, there is a third stratum of abstraction. Here sensible determinants are avoided altogether, and we work with concepts derived from intuitive insights into reality's universal constitutents—the basic being underlying everything finite. We label such conceptions, and attendant judgments, transcendental (multi-representational), signifying that they mentally grasp a common core marking each existing entity, despite generic and specific differences. This distinctive discipline, or most intellectual realm, has been termed metaphysics (mainly ontology) traditionally—a strictly deductive knowing process, though still related to concrete referrents. It analyzes and explains reality's most fundamental features: the ultimate, objectively ascertainable import of essence and existence.[17]

The conceptions and judgments thus obtained reflect, by outlining more or less clearly, the original systematizing sources implicit in, hence supporting, our mediate (generic-specific) and proximate (particularized) understanding concerning empirically given things. They accordingly afford us a rational (not rationalized or subjectively projected) awareness regarding reality's intelligible foundations—its intrinsic integrity, consistency, and continuity. These qualities are seen as being's primordial essential characteristics. The existential element cannot be similarly analyzed, due to its tremendous complexity. We simply apprehend that vitalizing vector as the complementary more specialized actualizing force (with proportionate potential) for prior essential more generalized actualizing capacities.[18]

Since the metaphysical attributes garnered through conceptual judgments at this highest abstractive level have universal extension, they do not identify exactly with any concrete contingent subject. A proper proportionality or radical relevance does hold between the qualities and their multitudinous representatives, however, which relationship is classified as analogous. Such a real if imperfect connection exerts a unifying influence in two essential directions. It not only extends downwards and outwards (naturally), but inwards and upwards (supernaturally) also. The implications thereof thus testify to the ultimate coherence of all finite agents exemplifying the pertinent traits. They likewise link those dependent and limited participants in these ordered natural resources (on a graduated generic and specific scale) with a supernatural Source expressing them perfectly.[19]

The latter basic principle-agent relation obviously exceeds the proper proportionality analogy. Properly speaking, finite and infinite are incommensurable. A real though remote bond does hold here, as regards the former anyway; because the being (entitive existence) then contingently possessed fundamentally derives from and depends upon its absolute Author, consequently must somewhow reflect that Being's integrity. We may reasonably designate this definitive integrative impression a "pointer" proportionality. It indicates a dimly discerned, shadowy proportionality: pointing toward an Originator of finite being Who is Being supremely and inconceivably. The drastic ontological disparity characterizing such a relationship ordinarily receives a negative explanation—denying the former's limitations (essential multiplicity and existential contingency).[20] Yet mainly emphasizing what might be named an excluding approach appears as rather disconcerting for the knower. Simply removing restrictions on Being hardly helps promote human understanding, much less interest. Stressing the positive or perfective aspects, despite the effort's enormity (considering the totally transcendent), seems to provide a better alternative. That continually expanding challenge surely should prove more instructive and productive, both in understanding and loving, thereby insuring a fuller sharing of being.

NOTES

1. J. Maritain, *The Degrees of Knowledge,* 4th ed., G. Phelan, trans., (New York: Scribner's, 1959), p. 109.
2. "Little Errors in the Beginning," M. J. Adler, *The Thomist* 38 (Jan-

uary 1974): p. 39. Excerpts reprinted by permission of *The Thomist.* Cf. Maritain, *Knowledge,* pp. 91–95, 107–109.

3. Ibid., p. 41.

4. Ibid., p. 43.

5. Cf. W. Soffer, "Kant on the Tutelage of God and Nature," *The Thomist* 45, (January 1981): 38–40.

6. W. J. Hill, *Knowing the Unknown God* (New York: Philosophical Library, 1971), p. 4.

7. Adler, "Little Errors," pp. 43–46; Maritain, *Knowledge,* pp. 90–99.

8. Maritain, *Knowledge,* pp. 112–118; Cf. J. Maritain, *Existence and the Existent,* L. Galantiere, and G. B. Phelan, trans. (New York: Pantheon, 1948), pp. 80–84.

9. Maritain, *Degrees of Knowledge,* pp. 146ff. Cf. T. de Chardin, *The Phenomenon of Man,* trans. B. Wall (New York: Harper and Row, 1959), chapter 2; J. Huxley, *Religion without Revelation,* rev. ed. (New York: Harper, 1957), p. 41.

10. Maritain, *Degrees of Knowledge,* pp. 90–100; Hill, *Unknown God,* pp. 4–16.

11. Maritain, *Degrees of Knowledge,* pp. 90–100; 119–128; Hill, *Unknown God.*

12. Maritain, *Degrees of Knowledge;* Hill, *Unknown God.*

13. Maritain, *Degrees of Knowledge,* pp. 32–50, 202–205.

14. Ibid., pp. 32–50, 52–66.

15. Ibid.

16. Ibid.

17. Ibid., pp. 210–218.

18. Ibid.

19. Ibid.

20. Ibid.; Hill, *Unknown God,* pp. 17–22; 147–148.

Chapter Four

ANTHROPOLOGICAL RAMIFICATIONS

The foregoing traditional epistemological enlightenment, founded upon faith in humans' ability to understand reality objectively, has a profoudly liberating effect. It frees these so truly personally interpreted subjects from a predominantly sensible, material, natural bind. This is not entirely the case, of course, since they always are partly bound by their essential corporeal connections. Nevertheless, they here appear as enjoying an inherent, temporally and spatially transcendent, spiritual capacity, which affords them an understanding (and a loving) link with all finite beings, especially their own type. It similarly innately inclines them toward accepting a superior sustaining supernatural realm, underlying and overseeing everything. Thus cognitively and affectively disposed, at least potentially, they can consciously recognize and respect a possible supernatural revelation concerning reality's ultimate Source. Such distinctively personal intimations and inclinations do not depend upon formal philosophical education either; anymore than one must be sociologically and psychologically trained before becoming aware of his or her human condition. The latter, and other, further liberating disciplines (when truly objectively derived and rightly subjectively applied) certainly aid personal development; insofar as they adequately acknowledge the real priority of substantial-spiritual, along with sensible-corporeal, reception over its subsequent extended construction and projection.[1]

Momentarily delaying attention to additional advantages that follow from this principally objectively, and proportionately substantially or spiritually, structured epistemological outlook, we may profitably consider some implications it holds for faith. As observed previously, faith's cognitive contents comprise very general fundamental assumptions regarding reality. They represent relatively intuitive insights (implicit judgments) concerning ultimate meanings, stimulated and supported by connected but incomplete indicators. Faith consequently involves a more or less advance identification with an unknown, facilitated through the spontaneous mental synthesis (subjectively and objectively) which the pertinent evidence prompts. Such an integral conception then produces a complementary vital reaction crucially influencing (guiding) subsequent thought and practice.[2] Faith is not really inductively or indirectly attained, therefore, properly or systematically speaking. Quite the contrary, it is directly achieved, or rather received—from intrinsically compelling (humanly intelligible) tangential testimony.[3] The resultant belief (postulate, presumption, dogma, wisdom-sapientia), and preliminary knowledge (scientia) attendant upon the same testimony (founding hope), inspire and integrate ensuing efforts at testing the thesis. Thence come the deductive and inductive endeavors manifesting the latter's latent import; accordingly aiding its fuller interpretation and evaluation. Those relevant correlations necessarily demand increasingly penetrating reflection, with corresponding authoritive objective assistance, as one's level of living intensifies. Holistic faith, enabling an individual to be a person—by living ever more satisfyingly or substantially beyond mainly material, naturally or corporeally confined means, under authentic supernaturally revealed spiritual auspices—surely shows superiority over the spiritually subverted, sensibly substituted humanly concocted, ideologic type.

Humans' near limitless capacity for understanding concrete reality—ultimately or universally, mediately or generically-specifically, and proximately or particularly—testifies convincingly to their principally spiritual status. Through such cognitive (and complementary affective) identification with the objective-subjective aspects of empirically given entities, while concomitantly maintaining yet proportionately expanding each so endowed agent's own individual-personal identity, they decisively demonstrate supra–sensible-corporeal powers.[4] Those especially characteristic substantive-qualitive resources, though immanently participating the infinite, are intrinsically finite and contingent. They receive existence fundamentally, as also the supplemental assistance needed in advancing toward its, and the accompanying essence's, possible completion—understanding and loving. That spiritual dependency is further indicated by human nature's inherent link to matter—an inferior but vitally required co-principle (spatial-temporal). Only through the latter, which the former activates and properly dominates, can the thus consolidated being adequately develop. So basically blended, and innately dynamically (perfectingly) or historically (freely) situated—amid aiding physical-biological (and angelic) counterparts—humans struggle more or less successfully at attaining fulfillment.[5]

In the course of learning much concerning themselves and the environment, via shared experimentation and reflection, accordingly freely fostering their duly autonomous developmental process, they continually confront a most crucial vital problem. It entails an experienced demand, subjectively and objectively, or individually-personally and collectively-communally, for ultimate standards (values and norms) that will supply a substantial-spiritual stabilizing framework both supporting and stimulating solid (durable) progress as regards understanding and loving. This essential exigency is therefore peculiarly pertinent to human relationships, promising a better balance (stressing quality over quantity) between freedom and responsibility, or diversity within unity. It necessarily bears upon other concrete connections also, although rather indirectly or vicariously. Such awareness stems from an enhanced consciousness of the elementary reality (basic being) underlying humanity's essential content. Increasing involvement with freedom's personalizing implications—impelling the mind toward a more integral vital viewpoint, wherein action's effect is seen as influencing both subject and object on a greater or lesser holistic scale—sharpens one's ontological (metaphysical) outlook. The self's and others' overall or qualitive aspects then become proportionately important when making decisions to promote possible advantages. Consistency and continuity consequently assume pronounced significance; whether touching longer or shorter-range relations. All are envisioned as concertedly assisting an abiding individual-personal and social-communal completion—total human development.[6]

Efforts at devising some sort of unifying system for human affairs, through strictly natural rational endeavors, manifest serious substantial defects. This is the case cognitively, certainly, hence inevitably impede their complementary affective contributions, likewise substantively considered. Howsoever high the initial analytic assumptions (the low-level synthetic sort intrinsically lack capacity except supplementally) and careful the ensuing, existentially checked deductions, they invariably fail in affording adequate fundamental standards. Humanity's essential complexity—extensiveness and intensiveness (blending the biologic and the angelic, corporeal and spiritual)—surpasses its members' earnest interpretive abilities. They ever fall short of achieving a reasonably convincing, as aptly balanced, conceptual coverage, especially on the profoundly pertinent suprasensible plane. That frustrating fact surely shows clearly from such efforts' failure to produce a moral system that has been found theoretically acceptable and practically workable, in a more than regional cultural area. Accordingly, none has spawned, much less sustained, a truly organic, universal social order affecting life as a whole.

Two traditional, uncharacteristically human tendencies have exerted an evident impact insuring these results. One displays a decidedly exaggerated (pseudoangelic) penchant for the abstract or absolute. It would turn human nature "inside out," or make it entirely pseudospiritual. By excessively emphasizing, and so simplifying, reality's unifying objective features, its proponents would make merely elementary standards, conveniently pragmatically supplemented, sufficient guidelines toward meeting humanity's dynamic needs. Obviously, this angelistic, idealistic, superstitious approach cannot carry reasonable conviction under human nature's essentially and existentially complicated vital conditions. Contrarily, a perennially prevalent preoccupation with the easily available and readily adaptable, sensible, so-called empirical, subjective aspects of reality (because the copious, "freely" captivating benefits gained appear most plausible, principally numerically viewed) has historically tended to turn human nature "outside in." It would make the latter entirely pseudo-corporeal. That more popular secular stress, reflecting a "sophisticated" animalistic or radically romantic attitude, represents the "substitious" stance—whether sheerly sensualistic or supposedly scientific, discussed previously. Following either artfully wileful and willful ideologic way, humans become only helplessly compromised creatures. Individual, largely subjective-corporeal interests actually prevail over communal, properly personal, objective-spiritual obligations—overtly and honestly, or covertly and hypocritically.[7]

Since human nature, adequately integrally considered, really reflects an essentially and existentially unique (generic-specific-particular or spiritual-corporeal) participation in universal contingent being, the concrete agents who actually comprise it must look for light regarding ultimate values and norms as basically flowing from their foundational source. A cognitively balanced—objectively and subjectively—metaphysics finds finite being fundamentally founded upon an infinite originating and sustaining Principle. The former also discovers this supertranscendent Absolute to be a self-subsisting spiritual or Personal Being. Recognizing the diverse created types—especially the human—as inherently albeit necessarily imperfectly revealing qualities of the Creator, such a superscience likewise indicates a correspondingly intrinsic possibility that a further fuller revelation concerning humanity's creaturely role might well be given the latter.[8]

Though humans have an innate inclination toward the supernatural, through their natural universalizing or transcending capacities, they cannot "possess a preliminary law of that which can and is to be revealed," Rahner reminds us. Possessing merely a very vague and elementary awareness along those transcendental lines at best, these cognitively limited subjects must receive enlightening assistance there even more than on the regularly experienced living level. Nevertheless, he adds, we may reasonable anticipate certain key revelatory characteristics because they will accord with the recipients' natural facilities. Otherwise the message's crucial content could hardly be known and respected.[9]

Thus, one might rightly expect an additional revelation to make much use of the word, as this constitutes the addressees' main communicating medium. It would then implicitly (or correctly) emphasize their reasoning or chief cognitive power; if it (word) were originally really objectively obtained, not simply subjectively, hence actually affectively, rationalistically constructed. Similarly, a strong stress on overt action should mark such a telling contribution rather evidently, thereby meeting human nature's subsequent complementary, not initial declaratory, essential expressive (constructive-projective) needs. Exalting societal or organic social relationships above individual interests appears as another vitally important aspect. Humans' basic bent that way for fulsome growth consequently becomes better realized. An authentic supernatural revelation can scarcely avoid adopting a progressively phased announcing approach, adjusted to the receivers' historically conditioned assimilative and responsive abilities. Lacking advance intimations and preparations, the likelihood of the latters' amenability, beyond the curious and the spurious, is surely weak. This evolutionary requirement —entailing inner consistency and continuity amid outer change, or integral development, as regards the revelation's impact—necessarily applies *ex post facto* also, given humanity's natural expansive dynamism.[10] Probably the contribution carrying utmost ultimate significance, in establishing the fundamental values and norms undergirding all human standards, would be the answers such supernatural revelation affords the critical questions bearing upon human nature's essential dynamic meaning—its "why," "what," and "how." Equally pertinent here, undeniably, would be possible insights concerning the vital connection between those foundational features and their Absolute Author.[11]

NOTES

1. "Subjectivists are made, they are not born. The non-professional . . . is an extreme realist; he is . . . deeply impressed with the objectivity of thought and . . . naturally certain that thought attains an other than thought."—J. F. Peifer, *The Mystery of Knowledge* (Albany: Magi Books, 1964), pp. 11–12.
2. A. R. Gini, "William James," pp. 499ff.
3. Rahner, *Foundations of Christian Faith.*
4. Ibid., pp. 35–39. Cf. also K. Rahner. *Hearers of the Word,* M. Richards trans. (New York: Herder and Herder, 1969), pp. 37–38.
5. Rahner, *Foundations of Christian Faith,* pp. 116–117, 121–129, 130–140.
6. Ranher, *Foundations of Christian Faith,* pp. 37–43.
7. Maritain, *Degrees of Knowledge,* pp. 14–16; Rahner, *Hearers of the Word,* pp. 25–27.
8. Rahner, *Hearers of the Word,* pp. 86–93, 103–108. Cf. also Maritain, *Degrees of Knowledge,* pp. 231–236.
9. Rahner, *Hearers of the Word,* pp. 112–120.
10. Ibid., pp. 154–161; Rahner, *Foundations of Christian Faith,* pp. 153–162.
11. Rahner, *Hearers of the Word,* pp. 167–169.

Chapter Five

SUPERNATURAL REVELATION'S HISTORY

1. Humanity's capacity for a supernatural revelation derives from a "built-in" spiritual dimension. That suprasensible resource includes the cognitive power not only to penetrate the generic and specific or natural aspects of its own essential content, along with the similar qualities of other finite types (thereby facilitating a certain existential control over all), but likewise to grasp the universal, metaphysical or quasi-supernatural factors (the being) underlying and unifying these empirical entities. Consequently, humans can envision the latters' radical contingency and decisive dependency on a self-subsisting supporting Source. Since this elemental insight shows the entire extensive panorama as really revealing the Creator's continuous gracious assistance, the so enlightened subjects concomitantly recognize the possibility of additional helpful manifestations being received. Such a vaguely conceived theoretical potential actually assumes profound practical relevance. Tremendously reinforced by fabulously frustrating experience with human nature's historical, critical disorderly inclinations (individually and collectively considered), further supernatural intervention seems to be an inherent necessity. Both cognitive processes—the simpler, more intuitive, theoretical, and

the more complex, instinctive, practical, considered earlier, are evident in the religious and ethical-philosophical traditions characterizing all people. Those customs thus reflect a certain supernatural awareness and involvement. What decisively distinguishes them, truly humanly viewed, is their basic causal or developmental balance.

As we observed previously, the crucial vital component determining whether humans' dynamic relationships (self-wise and otherwise) maintain a proper order—objectively and subjectively or substantially and supplementally—consists of these formally blended agents' spiritual-corporeal constitution. The resultant consciously consolidated structural interpretation—cognitively, representing that integrated central condition—psychologically, provides the key to rationality for this unique creaturely nature. Lacking this fundamental insight concerning humanity's formal causal content—its essential ''what'' (founded on faith), the then unbalanced, superficial believer remains seriously confused, when knowing and doing (understanding and loving). Such latent confusion shows quite patently through the subsequent misconceptions offered regarding human nature's proportionately relevant final cause—its essential ''why,'' as also the corresponding functional one—its essential ''how.'' The distortion thereafter becomes enormously compounded by ensuing extended connecting correlations.

We have already noted the pseudorationality or rationalizing strategy prevailing among devotees of the modern ''substitious'' (substitutional) scientific attitude. Either outrightly denying, or obliquely disparaging, reality's spiritual, substantially systematizing, vitalizing import, even on the profoundly probative human plane, those secularized professionals cleverly construct and project a mainly material or corporeally construed natural order. Arbitrarily assuming that sensible data alone is objectively available or reliable (subverted faith), its adherents automatically presume a mutual admirational and social inspirational, knowledgeable status. They compete and campaign (individually or collectively) in devising and developing theories that logically synthesize sensible-empirical evidence, mustered along largely quantitive, marginally qualitive (material or corporeal) lines. Professional plausibility—derived from peer and popular acceptance of technically proficient proof (''by the numbers'' or pragmatically coherent ''wonders'')—constitutes the ultimate verifying criterion.

Obviously, any openings for supernatural contacts are rather solidly sealed off here, as ''rationally'' unthinkable. Some so ''enlightened'' scientists—the sociologists examined earlier—emulating Kant, may allow or perhaps advocate a certain continuing connection with the former, indirectly at least and independently (no divine disclosure, merely human discovery). Such a subjectively sponsored effort appears grim—defensively composed, and thin—autonomously imposed, spiritually speaking. It markedly resembles Luther's convenient conscientious attitude, however, supposedly insuring against possible supernatural risks, while simultaneously assuring actual natural autonomy. A moral system is contrived in much the same rationalistic vein as the physical-biological one, and the ''supernatural'' ranked alongside but after the natural order. The former accordingly amounts to another self-asserting and satisfying accomplishment aiding romantically ''enlightened'' human advancement. This scientific charade really represents a not very subtle attempt at covering up the fact that the corporeal ''cart'' has been placed before the spiritual ''horse.''

Consequent upon such ''substitious'' (substitutional) conceptions concerning human nature's structural or formal import, correspondingly distorted interpretations of its purposeful or final and procedural or functional components inevitably follow. The latter sensibly prominent and pertinent dynamic factor receives dominant attention, ostensibly outranking its properly prior and controlling (in a truly objectively rational view) counterparts. As we learned from our foregoing sociological survey, practical or overt action is conceived to be the principal force determining human and all vital development. Self-realization through self-expression allegedly epitomizes every organism's existence. Structures and purposes are simply subsidiary mechanisms—staging "platforms" and stimulating "targets," facilitating finer functions. Action thus occurs chiefly for action's sake because "happenings" mainly make life worthwhile.

Parsons was seen earlier explaining the human dynamism on a cybernetic basis. Data of various kinds, more or less logically arranged, becomes absorbed by the individual organism, giving it a seemingly "knowledgeable" responsive capacity. Under appropriate pressure or stimulus at different organic levels, somewhat marginally selected answering contributions are constructed and projected. A rather robotlike rationality therefore prevails, diversified and distinguishable largely in accordance with higher physical-biological or sociological conditions (Parsons's "environments"), subjectively and "objectively" considered. The relativizing behaviorism and historicism that results theoretically interprets those reactions mainly as socially constituted reflexes. Reduced to such prominently spontaneous, practically instinctive, predominantly extraneously sparked status, freedom entails making more quantitive, technical, corporeally refined and confined choices.

This sharply sensibly slanted attitude toward human activity supports the plausibility notion of "knowledge" expounded by Berger, as indicated before. Since spontaneity and sensitivity supposedly primarily characterize individual and societal involvements, information that readily promotes those inherent inclinations ordinarily acquires rapid, widespread approval. Because human nature is envisioned on a pronouncedly biological basis there, either explicitly or implicitly, quantitive (corporeal supplemental) fragmenting aspects are automatically accentuated over qualitive (spiritual-substantial) unifying ones. External appearance consequently counts more than internal significance when assaying vital worth. A credibility deriving from such large-scale but shortsighted acceptance accordingly reflects and aptly protects humans' perverse preference for a superficial, subverted liberty.

The somewhat private career competition among professionals mentioned previously becomes magnified greatly through their desire to meet the public-interest challenge existing here. Collaborating closely with the communications media-masters, formally or informally, these diverse scientific and artistic specialists provide the data (practical and theoretical) that feeds the "cybernetic circuits" activating countless individuals and groups. This continuing educational process, both academic and endemic—mass outlets, as it operates regularly amid a "Western" modern milieu, aims at cultivating consummately "enlightened," autonomously choosing and expressing, societal subjects. In Berger's opinion, that means the latter should be "heretics," allegedly acting independently, on the basis of the commonly available and plausible information imbibed.[1] Employing ever increasingly mechanized, hence materialized, techniques and tactics, however, besides chiefly corporealized topics—finer honed or higher biological themes, the said "substitious" (substitutional) system (representing rigidly naturalistic beliefs) contributes mightily to the artificial "cybernetic" freedom outlined above.

Such a subverting, secularizing, romantically ideological attitude toward the traditional Western holistic cultural order, founded for the most part upon an objectively acknowledged religious, or supernaturally given spiritual-moral reality, constitutes the so-called scientific enlightenment's human hallmark. Its vaunted "open market" mentality, when legally limited, has produced a certain tolerable balance between the individualistically oriented participants. Yet its temporally, tangibly acquisitive excesses have vicariously spawned a cleverly contrived, purportedly popular-protective, acquisitive alternative. This relatively recent, covert, yet ultraindividualistic development—civic control (total, universal) by select public masters, appears disguised as "scientific socialism" or collectivism. Those theoretically united but practically divided professional "leaders" especially exploit the "cybernetic" informational approach in guiding their followers. Though stridently stressing a superstitious, idealistically ideological unity (biological-sociological), they too foster "heresy," or choice according to Berger; so long as it promises improvements along corporeally plausible lines.[2] True, some significant differences set these directing and deciding process apart—the "scientific" socialistic idealism and the "scientific" individualistic romanticism. The distinctions are more supplemental than substantial however, quantitive rather than qualitive.[3] Both bodily based and bound beliefs overtly exemplify the standardized contrasting societal consequences of a "revelation" regarding humanity, and reality as a whole, derived from modern Western rationalistic and naturalistic discovery (idealism and romanticism).

2. Despite this modernistic scientific influence, which has been exported by the "West" around the world, Asian and African religious-ethical philosophical thought and practice still mainly manifest their own traditional insights and interpretations concerning the natural-supernatural connection. They thus contribute respectively to revelation's historical meaning. Displaying notably contrary psychological propensities within a common human framework, each exerts a complementary balancing impact upon Western, typically rationalistic and scientific tendencies. Nevertheless, since such exotic attempts at religio-ethical enlightenment also are principally naturally founded—glimpses of the "above" garnered from "below," they likewise evidence serious deficiencies. As we will see subsequently, those ultimate, transcendental or metaphysical endeavors incline toward what we may term superstitious excesses.

Starting with the Asian experience, several important clarifications should be made. We must first distinguish between East

Asians and West Asians. The former chiefly reflect membership in the Mongoloid primary race or racial stock (physically and culturally). The latter largely show similar Caucasoid origins.[4] Those markedly distinctive peoples' philosophical-religious outlooks accordingly exhibit correspondingly different characteristics. When talking about Oriental customs, we must realize that it is the East Asians to whom we rightly refer. West Asian habits are not properly included then, strictly anthropologically speaking, for the most part anyway. This fundamental natural fact frequently, if not usually, receives little recognition by commentators upon the Indian cultural scene, especially its religio-moral aspects. Situated at the Caucasoid area's eastern extremity, Indians inevitably portray some Oriental influence. Nevertheless, their more typical theoretical and practical patterns—ethical-philosophical speculation quite prominently—depict a decidedly rational (reasoning), Western or Occidental attitude.[5]

S. Radhakrishnan, the widely known and respected Indian philosopher, explains how Indian religion emphasizes a rational, synthesizing approach, utilizing advances in experimental data. He also mentions the fact that the general impression of a philosophy rather than a religion conveyed by Hinduism further accentuates its rational import.[6]

Even on the ordinary popular plane, the caste, karma, and reincarnation ideals bear a basic reasonable implication, despite radical exaggeration. They indicate an inherent inclination toward establishing a systematic social order together with a belief in moral commitment as the crucial means facilitating one's eventual arrival at a better personal state.[7]

The "mainline" Oriental religious or ethical-philosophical representatives are found among East Asians—the Chinese (Confucianism, Taoism, Buddhism), the Japanese (Shintoism, Buddhism), and the remaining Mongoloid membership who principally have adopted Buddhism. Confucianism, Taoism and Shintoism evidence a close resemblance—concerning ends and means certainly—though Taoism differs sharply as regards methods. Each advocates self-fulfillment through adjustment to an ideal moral order. The latter believes this follows largely from absorption in an underlying universal cosmic order, however, rather than the conscious practice of virtue, like the former. Confucianism and Shintoism stress virtuous action socially: by family, friendly, and political loyalty.[8] All three thus offer a mainly, if not entirely, naturalistic (hence heavily materialistic) intuitively rational anthropocentric revelation therefore. While Taoists emphasize individual personal completion—the perfectly wholesome person—Confucianists and Shintoists seek ultimate satisfaction via noble sociability.[9]

Buddhism reflects a somewhat similar self-sublimating and so supposedly saving ethical process. Humans' essential capacities can be actualized only under a self-induced enlightenment, it says. Such an exalted condition entails exorcising the phenomenal-empirical consciousness, thereby facilitating release into an ''unconditioned'' or nonreasoning, blissful state. One then gains greater understanding and appreciation of the self, as well as everything else.[10] Here too we have a chiefly naturalistic, strongly—even explicitly materialistic, intuitively rational anthropocentric revelation. Rather resembling Confucianism, it does demand virtuous effort—mental and moral discipline, for fostering final fulfillment—nirvana. Like the former also, these values and norms are very vague or fundamental, leaving their practical interpretation and application to individually enlightened insights.[11] Not surprisingly, Buddhism never achieved acceptance, either extensively or enduringly at least, in its native India. The sharply subjective, purportedly intuitive implications thereof presumably conflicted radically with the Indians' more objective, rational (reasoning), and ritually organized, religious-ethical attitude.

3. Diversity and virility aptly characterize traditional African religions. Supernatural intensity—recognizing ultimate dependence upon divine support—constitutes another dominant trait.

Those religious qualities apparently derive from the native Africans' general social tendencies.[12] The close connection between such inclinations is readily evident—

> There is no African tribe whose life is not surrounded and penetrated by rites and rituals. Such events as birth and death, initiation and marriage, planting and harvesting, drought and rain are freighted with symbolism, finding visible expression in accompanying cults and customs. The invisible background of this symbolism consists of different myths that connect the particularities of life with the totality of being . . . the semantic thrust of African mythology [is] that God is presence, continuing providence, mysterious power, in all things, the one because of whom man is capable of acting and is morally responsible for what he is doing.[13]

Summarily considered, then, the historical religious faith of Negroid Africa presents a pronounced contrast to its Oriental counterpart. Besides being basically divinely or supernaturally directed, the former includes a decidedly practical, empirical, prominently instinctively rational personal approach for preserving and promoting that relationship. Contrarily, the latter remains largely, nearly totally, naturally and humanly bound despite a highly abstruse, intuitively idealistic, ethical-philosophical outlook. Orientals stress self-completion principally through intellectual concentration, focussing attention on requisite moral norms merely minimally or marginally. Africans especially emphasize multi-ritual, socio-moral obligations, as more or less mystical methods that alone insure proximate security and ultimate personal integrity. The differences at issue here reflect opposing bents toward predominantly contemplative and active living respectively.[14] Oriental perfection entails a rather profoundly passive, intensely introverted, individualistic condition, supplementally manifested by scrupulous observance of traditional customs. African fulfillment is achieved solely via a wholehearted participation in the socially established and strictly enforced specific ethical patterns. Such rules and rituals are mainly peculiar to, hence traditionally synonymous with, each tribe.

Two points made previously, when commencing these revelatory comparisons, can now be understood better. The relatively polar psychological attitudes (intuitively versus instinctively rational) characterizing the Oriental and African religio-ethical positions respectively exert a counterbalancing influence upon the more comprehensively rational (reasoning) Western or Occidental stance. Obviously, those variations represent distinctions of degree only, since the subjects exhibiting them possess the same fundamentally rational human nature. They indicate mutually complementary essential racial traits, or what might aptly be termed species-proportionality, displayed by the human genus. Because the several contrasting cognitive-affective, or interpretive and expressive approaches to reality entail principally natural inherent inclinations and actual accomplishments, they share a common ultimate deficiency—short-sightedness. Even though they may admit, and allegedly accept, supernatural assistance (Orientals and Africans anyway), more or less explicitly, connections therewith remain veiled and vague, if not contradictory, at best. While true insights possibly occur, momentarily and fragmentarily, seeking the supernatural chiefly through transcendent natural personal experience and expression constitutes the "bootstrap lifting" operation par excellence. It inevitably involves superstition—radically identifying the spiritual with the corporeal. Formally or substantially considered, then, that revelation does not differ very much from the scientifically enlightened, "substitious," Occidental kind—where the corporeal is substituted for the spiritual. Relative responsibility differs drastically, however, as the latter have forsaken a previously and proximately given, especially elevating (supernatural) enlightenment.

Recalling earlier remarks regarding reasonably expectable aspects of a supernatural revelation, it seems appropriate to measure typical Oriental and African religio-ethical attitudes against them. We noted that enlightenment by the objectively given and guiding word—stimulating rational intelligible response—should be a prominent revelatory feature. Only such a crucially cognitive contact could aptly activate the human agent. Oriental world views certainly employ explanatory efforts along these thematic lines, but quite loosely and obtusely. Their metaphysical conceptions are largely subjectively derived, founded upon individual introspection. They do not reflect something received so much as report discoveries concerning natural experience. This accordingly represents enlightenment through attempts at profound self-analysis. The African ultimate understanding, undeniably objectively oriented and stimulated, discloses a decidedly spontaneous reaction to reality's meaning. It rather entails instantaneous insights and interpretations, consequently likewise strongly subjectively slanted, yet allowing more openings for supernatural import. They receive and respect a revealed word mainly by manifesting deeds relatively remotely recognizing the metaphysical and the divine in a concrete corporeal context.[15]

A clearly discernible consistency and continuity with prior preparatory and subsequent declaratory announcements was seen as another significant characteristic of a valid supernatural revelation. Oriental and native African naturalistic contributions surely exhibit a fundamental faithfulness toward historical traditions. Though the different doctrines and practices do evidence some serious disagreement, there is much basic similarity between them. Such linkages are possible, obviously, because the overall outlook remains much the same among the separate peoples. However, their theoretical simplicity, as regards vital values and norms, permit extensively varied practical interpretations and applications. Little or no organic unity invigorates the various traditions, hence systematic development cannot occur. They exist merely as schools—in the Orient, except where officially ritually adopted by governments or families. For the Africans, they amount to tribal or smaller groups' general customs, having no real integral identity as a coherent constructive societal force.[16]

We observed previously how human nature's essential expressive (active) inclinations would very likely receive additional relevant encouragement from a supernatural revelation. When comparing the relative active commitments that the Mongoloid and Negroid peoples' religio-ethical beliefs inspire, the latter apparently emphasize overt engagement more prominently than the former. Africans display a rather wide variety of personal social services carrying specific moral obligations. The Orientals insist instead upon a few crucial elementary practical duties (thus lessening interference with contemplation), further implemented chiefly through individually exercised discretion. Since the ultimate values supporting both types' normative standards are largely corporeally conceived—exorcising complexity (Orientals) and increasing security (Africans)—tangible, temporal benefits principally motivate compliance therewith. The resultant endeavors accordingly actually accentuate getting over giving to a great extent. This de facto functional identity, despite *de natura* dynamic differences, indicates the levelling effect exerted by the bodily bind. Africans manifest multiple communal loyalties, so long as they encompass somewhat small-scale, close-knit societal units. Orientals theoretically evidence a profound awareness of social reciprocity, embracing widespread membership—like the nation or even all mankind. Pragmatically, though, interest centers on the family, clan, or other local group, unless circumstantially compelled to accept broader tangible ties.[17]

As regards constructive social contributions—meaning their import for advancing societal development, neither the Mongoloid nor the Negroid religo-ethical standards have stimulated much concerted progress. Native African life has remained rather firmly fixed in the early clannish and tribal mold, except where revised under foreign influence (directly or indirectly). Orientals too have agelessly adapted their extremely simplified utlimate norms along relatively static, pragmatic collective lines. Only when "liberated" laterally from outside did they move beyond staid ethnic patterns that restricted cultural advances. Both peoples certainly exhibit impressive artistic, as well as some scientific and philosophic accomplishments, besides accompanying technical and political skills. These have tended toward a monotonous repetition, however, structurally and functionally, or qualitively considered. They thus seemingly reflect, not entirely but to a significant degree at least, the vital limitations that attend upon a heavily corporeally weighted, naturalistic religio-ethical revelation. Unfortunately, though, those two basic racial types have more recently made the mistake of adopting the easier, hence supposedly better, modernistically progressive alternative course—the "scientifically enlightened" Western way.[18]

Critically crippling defects in the last listed category concerning reasonably expectable revelatory characteristics encapsulate the Oriental and African religio-ethical weaknesses. Each has been bedeviled by the close connection between human nature's spiritual and corporeal components. Although such distinctions are usually recognized theoretically, what the concepts imply—differences of degree only (accidental), or kind (substantial)—normally remains unclear. This is a sure sign that the respective insights do not display a decisively supernatural import; since spirit's substantive quality, and its inherent dynamic autonomy, essentially identify the latter. Both exotic views accordingly evidence the same confused consequences—excessively emphasizing sensible factors (either positively or negatively)—somewhat like their naturalistically enlightened Occidental counterparts. While respectively indulging intrinsic personal proclivities—Mongoloids idealistically or intuitively stressing moral ends (finality), Negroids pragmatically or instinctively preoccupied with moral methods (function)—the two extremist approaches treat the crucial middle moral term (means or form) rather superficially. They tend toward accepting it as chiefly corporeal, therefore must employ largely superstitious notions to afford it purportedly supra-mundane significance. Natural and supernatural then become nearly indistinguishably entwined, inevitably causing misleading theoretical impressions and encouraging mistaken practical expressions.[19]

Those so handicapped people have received confirming, essentially compromised assistance, remotely or obliquely anyway, from the "substitious" scientific contributions exported by the extravagantly rationalistic Caucasoid communities. These, as the human type especially endowed for mediating or moderating service, having seriously subverted such natural talents, exercise a correspondingly confounding influence instead.[20] They pass along their perversely plausible theories and practices to all who do not possess a truly supernatural revelation capable of combatting them.

NOTES

1. Berger, *Heretical Imperative*.

2. Barbara Ward, *Faith and Freedom*, pp. 196–210.

3. C. Dawson, *The Judgment of the Nations* (New York: Sheed and Ward, 1942), pp. 186–197. G. Steiner, "The Lollipopping of the West," *New York Times*, Dec. 9, 1977 (Op-Ed page).

4. C. S. Coon and E. E. Hunt, *Living Races of Man* (New York: Knopf, 1965), p. 204.

5. R. C. Zaehner, *At Sundry Times* (London: Faber and Faber, 1958), pp. 35–36, 58–60.

6. I. S. Radhakrishnan, *Indian Philosophy*, R.A. McDermott, ed., as cited in *Radhakrishnan, Selected Writings on Philosophy, Religion and Culture*, (New York: E. P. Dutton, 1970), p. 70. Cf. A. C. Danto, *Mysticism and Morality* (New York: Basic Books, 1972), pp. 23–24.

7. McDermott, *Indian Philosophy*, pp. 187–221. Cf. Danto, *Mysticism*, pp. 27–31.

8. R. C. Zaehner, *The Catholic Church and World Religions* (London: Burns and Oates, 1964), pp. 70–71. Cf. K. Ch'en, *Buddhism in China* (Princeton, N.J.: University Press, 1964), pp. 21–27.

9. Zaehner, *The Catholic Church*, pp. 58–74. H. Kraemer, *World Culture and World Religions* (London, Lutterworth, 1960), pp. 174–175.

10. Zaehner, *The Catholic Church,* pp. 77, 81, 84–87. Kraemer, *World Culture,* pp. 158–159. Ch'en, *Buddhism,* pp. 4–10.

11. Ch'en, *Buddhism,* pp. 5–7.

12. H. Kraemer, *Christian Message in a Non-Christian World* (London: J. Clark and Co., 1946), p. 337. Cf. P. H. Gulliver, "Anthropology," *African World,* R. A. Lystad, ed. (New York: F. A. Praeger, 1965), p. 67.

13. W. Dupre, *Religion in Primitive Cultures* (Hague: Mouton, 1975), pp. 68–69. Cf. G. Parrinder, *African Traditional Religion,* 3rd ed., rev. (London: Sheldon Press, 1974).

14. E. Zolla, "Traditional Methods of Contemplation and Action," in *Traditional Modes of Contemplation and Action,* Y. Ibish and P. L. Wilson, eds. (Tehran: Imperial Iranian Academy of Philosophy, 1977), pp. 43–81.

15. M. Eliade, *Cosmos and History* (New York: Harpers, 1959), p. 3. T. Berry, *Five Oriental Philosophies* (Albany, N.Y.: Magi Books, 1968), pp. 15–30.

16. Berry, *Oriental Philosophies.* B. Davison, *The Africans* (London: Longmans, 1969), chapter 10.

17. Dupre, *Primitive Cultures,* pp. 67–75. F. Grant, *Oriental Philosophy* (New York: Dial Press, 1936), pp. 85–94, 163–182.

18. Berry, *Oriental Philosphies,* pp.. 43–46. Davidson, *The Africans,* pp. 111–117, 173–179.

19. K. Rahner, *Foundations of Christian Faith,* pp. 170–175.

20. See the Author's "Toward a Trinitarian Theology of Mission," in *Missiology,* (April 1981): 155–169.

Part III

Chapter Six

CHRISTIAN REVELATION

Checked against the foregoing reasonably discernible natural requisites for a humanly viable supernatural revelation, the Christian salvific message is seen as radically realistic.

First. It clearly accords the word top priority, making that the primary medium upon which everything else depends. It even personalizes this word, directly and divinely, identifying both message and messenger with the absolute supernatural Source thereof. Such living Word became humanly incarnate, we learn, being thus patently objectively given, and similarly subjectively received, or rejected, by the relatively autonomous addressees. Rather than coming from within those rational agents—through self-inspection, or from around them either—cosmic reflection, it ultimately transcends all, reinterpreting the whole in a more thoroughly meaningful light. The latter illuminates human nature much like an X-ray picture, exposing inner spiritual features while comparatively shading outer corporeal ones. Intuitive and instinctive extremes are avoided, as attention is focused on reasonable evaluation and responsible decision. Obligations, or obedience to higher and deeper common concerns, take precedence over lesser individual interests and inclinations. Wholesomeness (holiness)—quality controlling quantity, substantial-spiritual dominating the supplemental-corporeal, giving outranking receiving, constitutes the central ideal.[1]

Second. The Christian revelation proximately and profoundly continues, yet completes, the prophetic teachings of the lengthy Jewish religious history that preceded it. Christ regularly reaffirmed this fact, as further evidence regarding his credibility. Though a drastically new order was proclaimed, its implications were shown to consummate, not destroy, the old. He really presented himself as a religious reformer, therefore, not a revolutionary, despite the seeming radical revisionary import his ideas held for their recipients—especially many fabulously false Jewish leaders.[2]

Besides manifesting a close correlation with a specific preparatory supernatural disclosure, the Christian revelation displays a still stronger subsequent consistency and continuity. Consequent upon Christ, it entails an organic social entity or society (the kingdom of God developing). Recognizing humanity's intrinsic collective dimensions, and the historical element characterizing such nature's vital dynamism, Christianity's founder established the institution we term the Church. That concrete believing community, firmly, comprehensively erected—structurally as well as functionally, maintains a distinct identity, worldwide, amid other related but organically restricted corporate types. This religio-moral agency accordingly comprises much more than a theoretical "school" (among the Orientals), or practical tribal-political customs (among the Africans). It involves juridical-moral, corporeal-spiritual, or basically blended authoritive bonds, consonant with the temporal communal needs of its human constituents. On the same common count, graded relationships mark the membership at various levels in the system. Personally united to Christ—through his persistent personal presence, sacramentally and serviceably (doing "the will of the Father"), each one individually, and all together, advance toward the kingdom's ultimate fulfillment. The thus synthesized societal connections reflect and protect the said revelation's vital integrity, while simultaneously promoting or sharing it among those who wander outside its specifically saving scope.[3]

Third. Such a sharing commitment that marks, and helps make, the Christian revelation goes quite beyond the serving or self-denying role required by naturally inspired revelatory messages. Since the former envisions humans' spiritual component as at least a semiconcrete reality (full-scale concreteness essentially entails corporeal counterparts), self-denial is not mainly a negative attitude—release from excessive bodiliness. Service for others carries definite positive benefits, subjectively and objectively. The so active agent directly enhances his or her own spirituality, because the latter chiefly thrives through such genuine giving. Indirect advantages accrue in the assistance afforded individual beneficiaries and the common good, the promotion of whose welfare represents a loving return to them, and vicariously to God. These decidedly supernatural conceptions, with attendant expressions always founded upon faith, gradually become intense convictions, confirmed by constant reflective usage. The thus elevated persons increasingly understand and experience the crucial Christian truth that "the flesh is useless, the spirit gives life." They similarly see, and correspondingly enjoy, the value of "losing one's life" (degrading selfishness), and assuring its thorough attainment (divinizing otherness). This gospel-based and -developed, supernatural reasonableness ("what exchange will a man give for his soul?") ultimately culminates, temporally, in bodily death—completing the extended loving, "laying down of one's life" for friends. Then the enduring ennobled spirit enters upon an advanced but relatively passive supernaturally enlightening state, awaiting active sharing therein through reunion with a resurrected or glorified body. That rather succinctly summarizes the Christian revelation's personally invigorating import.[4]

Fourth. References regarding Christianity's contributions toward the Western world's social development were offered at the present study's start. Under its truly supernaturally inspired influence, the real constructive cultural gains already made by the peoples among whom the Church expanded achieved still greater development. Besides assuming more profound dimensions, they became better systematized and wider propagated along formal educational and religious institutional lines. Natural values and norms, correctly conceived, received further corroboration and intensification (theoretically and practically) from such supernatural connections. This insured greater clarity, certainty, and fuller extensions, as well as fostering less arbitrary or restrictive applications. Steadily, if not so easily, spreading across Europe, penetrating all social levels, barbarians and civilians alike gradually accepted and adjusted to its uplifting, unifying, dynamic impetus. Concerning Western cultural origins, Parkes says:

> The affirmations of Christianity . . . provided guidance and stimulation for aesthetic and intellectual exploration. These affirmations remained the basic postulates of Western thought even for men who repudiated the moral and theological claims of the Church. Supported by Christian faith in the unity and goodness of nature, in the value of the individual personality, and in the ultimate harmony of freedom and order, Western man began to create new political institutions establishing liberty under law, to produce literature and art that were increasingly infused with enjoyment of natural phenomena, and, in the course of time, to apply the concept of natural law to the understanding and control of natural forces.[5]

As we have seen previously too, the Western world has long since largely turned against this system, even though apparently retaining its preferred notions of personal freedom and social progress. Scientific-corporeal standards have been substituted for religious-spiritual ones, as the moral base upon which such secularized order rests. This is what the Western people did with the real supernatural enlightenment truly revealed to them. Besides paying ample penalties themselves, in rampant personal and social abuses, amid an overabundance of the latest, and allegedly highest (technologically speaking) living refinements currently available, they belittle traditional Oriental and African values by prodding those people toward adopting the same pseudosophisticated standards. As a patently and profoundly pertinent example, the former's population-planning wizards pay their native ''pied pipers'' of birth control among the latter, and so call the strictly technological ''tune'' that such social subverters very willingly (and wilefully) play. Here we have a classic case where the ''blind lead the blind''—both hooded and herded by the bodybind.

Fifth. That seriously ''comic'' situation exemplifies especially well how the Mongoloid and Negroid peoples' simplistic and superstitious tendency to identify the spiritual and the corporeal is craftily exploited under the Caucasoids' ''substitious'' scientific impact. We earlier noted the Orientals' prime focus on ends, with almost any methods (at least elementally moral) allowable for advancing them. We likewise found the Africans rather extremely emphasizing methods (morally and ritually) as automatically insuring individual and communal security. In each tradition, means carry significance merely instrumentally—facilitating favorable connections between the other two dynamic factors. This easily adjustable, two-dimensional approach dynamically (glossing over the middle term or form's consolidating import) invariably produces a single-dimensional interpretation regarding content—constitutionally. The concept of spirit is simply superimposed upon the bodily one, mythically or superstitiously. When the population-control strategy emanating from the Occident confronts these people, promising radical improvements over previous corporeal conditions, the natives have little reason or will to resist. Japan obviously offers a somewhat special submissive instance. Its traditional initiative in accepting and expertly applying foreign techniques that would assure tangible protection against natural material shortages (while still preserving a fundamental religio-ethical tradition) has made it a model for the contraceptive exponents. The same initiative has now nearly ''submerged'' it under Occidental culture.[6]

Stressing spirit, as an organically integral or semiconcrete vital state, represents the Christian revelation's crucial characteristic. That quality mainly marks a break with all other, supposedly divine dispensations—where spiritual and corporeal concepts reflect only differences of degree. Throughout the three complementary sectors comprising humanity's developmental dynamism (ends, means, methods), spirit decisively dominates. Thus, the Christian's faith concerning life's ultimate goal rests on the foundational fact (truth): "God is spirit."[7] God's very relevant relationship to them, sparking hope, follows from the additional crucial mediating fact (truth affecting all creaturely agents): "It is the spirit that gives life, the flesh is useless."[8] Completing the triple vital exigency, or overtly manifesting (as method) the two preceding basic facts, is another truth bearing a similar spiritual significance: "Those who worship [serve] him must worship [serve] him in spirit and truth." Stated more exactly, "Whosoever would save his life will lose it; whosoever loses his life . . . for the Gospel's sake will save it."[9]

Recognizing and respecting spirit's key role accordingly constitutes the cornerstone of the Christian vital edifice. This central supporting truth received correspondingly concerted emphasis during Christ's earthly ministry. He began his teaching by employing the theme: "Reform your lives; the kingdom of heaven is at hand."[10] Everything else said and done principally explained and exemplified what that decisive directive summarily implied—namely, reassert the spirit's proper dominion over the flesh. Only then would human nature regain its original formal balance, lost through a corporeally contrived compromise. Self-denial and other-avowal, giving more than getting, sacrificing tangible temporal sensible treasures for eternally enduring substantial ones, laying down bodily life along Gospel lines (the cross), so insuring permanent spiritual survival and ultimately a glorified corporeal revival; such are the formative measures whereby men and women attain eternal life. His message and mission were encapsulated in the epic exclamation—"I am the way, the truth, and the life."[11] The middle term of this saving "formula" carries crucial human import, reflecting Christ's chief mediating contribution—reformation. To the extent a person accepts and applies that corrective prescription, he or she becomes capable of performing the related requirements, following the way, promoting the proffered life. He proved its value, ultimately and communally, by his death and resurrection. He proves its value for us, proximately and personally, through our increasingly clear awareness of actually experiencing the promised life here and now, albeit imperfectly, while working toward its consummation.

Despite so much stress on explaining, and proportionate efforts at exemplifying spirit's preeminent vital role, many modernistic Christians (like earlier esoteric types) incline toward favoring a worldly-wise, body-wise compromise. Those "shortcut" specialists would in effect "work both ends" of Christ's salvific "formula" against the middle, apparently enjoying the spiritual and corporeal equally. They thus continually flout their Leader's warning that, "No man can serve two masters."[12] As a consequence, such obstinate deformers, rather than obedient reformers, develop what Christ called an "obtuse spirit."[13] Overextending externally the necessary balance between body and spirit, these sensibly slanted innovators become subconsciously subverted or compromised. Intellectual conception and volitional discretion endeavor to rationalize, hence seemingly justify, corporeal preferences. We accordingly find numerous so-called Christians approving abortion, contraception, homosexuality, pornography, radical sexual liberation, together with similar self-centered political-economic aberrations like pacifism and welfarism. Though often avidly advocated along allegedly moral lines, the latters' looseness and obtuseness exposes them as a clever cover for a pernicious body-bind. Their vociferous (frequently elegantly, even "elevatedly") exponents symbolize

Christ's advance admonition concerning the "kingdom" (Church) in this world—"The reign of God is also like a dragnet thrown into the lake, which collected all sorts of things."[14]

Only when the final historical moment arrives, and its climaxing event—the judgment of the nations, occurs, will the full and firm distinction (separating the spiritually living from the dead) be made. Existence beyond history, or drastically changing conditions, will then be the enduring state. Whoever have used the historical (with its prominent corporeal content) in due deference to the metaphysical (with its predominant spiritual imprint), all on a moderately balanced theological supernatural scale, will experience thoroughly eternal life (permanent vital order). Whoever have defied that essential and existential human balance, and thus defiled themselves, will experience eternal death (permanent vital disorder).[15]

NOTES

1. Rahner, *Foundations of Christian Faith*, pp. 223–225, 407–408.
2. Ibid., pp. 247–248.
3. Ibid., 326–346, 400–401. Cf. E. Schillebeck, *Christ, the Sacrament of the Encounter with God* (New York: Sheed and Ward, 1963), pp. 47–51.
4. Rahner, *Foundations of Christian Faith*, pp. 402–411, 435–441. Cf. K. Rahner, *On the Theology of Death*, C. H. Henkey, trans. (London: Nelson, 1961), Section I.
5. Parkes, *Gods and Men*, pp. 479. Excerpt from *Gods and Men: The Origins of Western Culture* by H.B. Parkes, copyright © 1969, by permission of Alfred R. Knopf, Inc. Cf. Dawson, *Western Culture*.
6. "How Japan Does It," *Time*, Vol. 117, No. 13 (March 30, 1981), pp. 54–60.
7. John 4:24 (All references are to the *New American Bible*, St. Paul Editions (Boston: Daughters of St. Paul, 1976).
8. John 6:63.
9. John 4:24; Mark 8:35.
10. Matt. 4:17.
11. John 14:6.
12. Matt. 6:24; Luke 16:15—"What man thinks important, God holds in contempt."

13. Mark 7:22.
14. Matt. 13:47.
15. Rahner, *Foundations of Christian Faith*, pp. 431–447.

Chapter Seven

CHRISTIAN REVELATION'S DYNAMIC IMPORT

The Christian revelation's unique superiority over other real and supposed supernatural dispensations has been seen as proved by its incisive manifestation of the spirituality characterizing God entirely, and humans predominantly. This intrinsic eminence is strengthened further through the telling vital ties that such revelation shows as marking humanity's blended constitution (spiritual-corporeal) and the fundamental developmental dynamism (ends, means, methods) impregnating all contingent beings. Both basic features consequently somehow reflect or project a living connection with, and dependence upon God, as Creator, Conserver, and Completor. Christ's key statement, summarizing His revealing, mediating role between God and mankind—"I am the way, the truth, and the life," definitively depicts those facts. It implicitly provides the crucial answers for the most profound questions regarding human nature—the "why," "what," and "how" controlling that creaturely condition. It therefore represents the adequately realistic personal response (objectively and subjectively, socially and individually, spiritually and corporeally) to these more or less autonomous agents' creative vital needs. Our ensuing investigative efforts must concentrate on explaining the Christian message's main meaning rather explicitly, and especially the societal ramifications thereof.

Modern psychology affords instructive insights concerning the central human dynamic, and so indirectly points toward Christ's ultimately suitable significance. Thus, psychoanalysis discerns a primordial covert dynamism activating the individual subject. Each person's innate developmental inclinations originate there. Thence spring the forces fostering growth, accordingly promoting self-realization or fulfillment. Jung classified such realm as the "unconscious." Freud recognized the same impelling source, terming it the "id."[1]

At the opposite dynamic extremity, both psychoanalysts distinguish another tellingly typical division in the human personality. This entails overt operating mechanisms enabling the agent to contact, and interact with, his or her environment. It contains varied practical procedures, reflecting a fundamental functional capacity for expressly giving and receiving. Being most specific or detailed, hence heavily sensibly weighted, they ordinarily make very vivid impressions upon their possessor. Jung and Freud each named that consumingly conscious and consummately mobile vital area the "ego."[2]

The same psychological specialists detect an additional, somewhat mediate, critical personal sector. Standards controlling usage of the different organs and faculties spawning and supporting the essential exigencies hold sway here. Those relatively central components, providing a certain living or balancing link between the foregoing contrasting tendencies, exert a consolidating influence that correspondingly structures or forms the subject, individually and socially. Jung saw it as the "semi-conscious" sphere, where the spiritual-corporeal, soul and body, principally adhere. Freud designated a similar semi-conscious, but strictly corporeal, formative category as the "super-ego."[3]

These thus decisively discernible subjective states, taken together, comprise the total human self or personality, in its elementary dynamic outlines. Rahner confirms such crucial vital capacities' existence from the theological viewpoint. He finds the "seminal person" to be "a continuing dimension of the one person, fulfilled in the 'achieved person,' via the 'intermediary reality of the person.' "[4] Each basic characteristic is interpreted developmentally or historically, as continuous complementary contributory constants, not simply total lifetime periods. Measured against the Christian revelation's supernaturally-lighted cosmic "screen," they show the "Trinitarian trace," or image here, unmistakably. Correctly, concertedly construed, and employed, their interlocked guiding (understanding) and guarding (loving) impact ("cognition" and "affect", according to Parsons) reflects (intimately and intricately) the divine dynamism's creative impress—as final, formal, and functional causes.[5]

The latter human distinctions represent the threefold personal manifestation (immanently) of the divinity's exemplarity (intelligibility-understanding) and efficiency (generosity-love), remotely certainly, or as projected "economically" (created). All three essentially coherent and cohesive, created personalized sectors consequently carry equal vital value. They therefore deserve a proportionately balanced (due priorities), progressively conscious, or humanly becoming recognition and respect. Envisioned as more proximate, hence better manageable and usable, succinct conditions, such critical substantive relationships rightly are seen as consecutively concerned with creatures' central dynamic components—ends, means, and methods. Whether we know it or not, it is under their stimulating and synchronizing influence that we constantly, if often inconsistently, seek satisfaction amid our manifestly multiple and complex engagements. This fundamental fact might be easier perceived when one recalls the persistently perplexing factors—why, what, how—which basically affect our efforts along those searching lines. Having a predominantly spiritual-substantial (theoretical-philosophical) significance, they require rather penetrating insight, or a readiness to probe beneath the largely corporeal-supplemental (practical-historical)—who, where, when—covering counterparts.

Before attempting additional elaborations on the theological theme of divine-human relations, some explanations regarding the divine life itself, derived from Christian revelation, are in order. The central truth characterizing the latter, and determining the message's entire content, discloses the ultimate supernatural reality, and mystery: God is perfect unity, yet simultaneously a personal Trinity. As already noted (in the immediately preceding reference), and generally known, we term the three Persons Who comprise the divine Trinity, Father, Son-Word, and Holy Spirit. Theologians traditionally have explained the commonly shared or unifying element between the distinct Persons as a single self-subsistent spiritual substance (intellect-will).[6] The distinguishing relationships within that foundational framework represent its essential activity. "The Father, Son and Spirit are identical with one godhead, and are 'relatively' distinct from one another . . . these opposed relativities are also concretely identical with both 'communications' ('Processions') as seen from both sides, through which the Father communicates the divine essence to the Son and through the Son to the Spirit, or through which the latter two receive (the same)."[7]*

Stated a little more personally perhaps, "the Father, Son and Spirit possess self-consciousness and each one is aware of the other two persons. But . . . this self-consciousness comes from the divine essence, is common as one to the divine persons, is therefore a characteristic moment of the concrete person."[8]

The three divine Persons thus inherently exercise intellection and volition, or understanding and love. The Father does so in uttering or begetting the Word-Son, and with Him spirating the Spirit. Both the Son-Word and the Holy Spirit respectively do this too, as proceeding from the Father. Each accordingly acts along relatively different, complementally linked, perfectly synthesized, spiritual lines.[9]

*This and following excerpts from K. Rahner, *The Trinity*, J. Donceel, trans. (New York: Harper, 1970) are reprinted by permission of the Winston-Seabury Press.

The Trinity's immanent substantial-spiritual (intellectual-volitional) unity exhibits three relational aspects therefore—the Father's begetting-originating, the Son-Word's proceeding-responding, the Holy Spirit's proceeding-responding. The second Person's response to the first Person's initiating contribution jointly spirates the third Person. The Latter's response consequently reflects that proportionately combined sharing. When projected "economically" or objectively—creating (conceiving, consolidating, completing), those almighty prerogatives constitute contingent reality's final, formal, and functional causes, objectively and ultimately. They impose the "Trinitarian trace" as mentioned above.

In the previous comment concerning the "Trinitarian trace" marking all creatures, such impress for humans was termed an image. This indicates the especially close connection human nature has with the divine nature originally. Its personalizing spiritual faculties (intellect and will), and more profoundly complex corporeal organs, clearly distinguishes it as a higher than merely physical-biological generic type. We thus note how "theologians discern a certain reflection of the Trinitarian process in the activity which the rational creature directs to himself. For in knowing himself the creature expresses an intelligible word which represents himself, and in the self-knowledge obtained in this word he loves himself; much as (Father) in the Trinitarian process expresses the Word which is an image of Himself, and through the Word breathes forth His love in the Holy Spirit."[10]

On the same relatively intimate, triadic symbolic score, we recall also the still stronger evidence indirectly supplied by modern psychology ("id," "super-ego," "ego"). Rahner's anthropological divisions ("seminal," "intermediary," "achieved") carry additional theological significance here too.

Accepting the foregoing theological explanations regarding the immanent Trinitarian relations, which characterize the Persons, we observe that the Son-Word possesses a certain mediating status. He "consolidates," one might say, the contrasting yet mutually complementary activity of the Father and the Holy Spirit. Analogously interpreted, or viewed against the human patterns considered above, His personal role rather resembles the middle component in our own cognitional and psychological syndromes. It accordingly appears as the "formulative," "evaluative" word ("semi-conscious"), linking the prior "covert conception" ("unconscious") with the subsequent "overt expression" ("conscious"). These divine relationships—thoroughly sharing the infinitely intimate and intricate, common spiritual substance—assuredly cannot change. Such a development would contravene God's absolute perfection. The same internal personal connections prevail, consequently, amid the Trinity's external, creative-redemptive engagements. As Rahner reminds us, God is not only "tri-personal" Himself ("Immanent Trinity"), but also communicates Himself "tri-personally" ("Economic Trinity").[11]

The latter communications (creation, redemption) follow from the three divine Persons' unified activity. They comprise one substantial Being, hence project their vital dynamism on that integral basis. Nevertheless, we may aptly attribute some special active influence to each Person, reflecting what we know of them through Revelation, and the Church's subsequent inspired interpretations. Guided by those traditional theological insights, then, we recognize the Father—the Trinity's originating Person, as likewise initiating-"conceiving" both creation's and redemption's plan. St. Paul evidently acknowledges this foundational fact when stating, "God (Father) chose us in him (Christ, the Son-Word incarnate) before the world began . . . he likewise predestined us through Christ Jesus to be his adopted sons . . . God has given us the wisdom to understand fully . . . the plan he was pleased to decree in Christ."[12]

Employing our human analogy again, we note how every plan chiefly aims at attaining a predetermined goal. Being largely a theoretical conception, that principal, purposeful or finalizing, dynamic factor implicitly includes everything required for the plan's fulfillment. The ''everything'' mentioned here mainly entails means or structures, and methods or functions, facilitating the end's achievement. These are merely ideally contained there, though, awaiting additional action promoting their development, as aiding the plan's objective realization. The Father, we believe, has proposed such a ''plan,'' with the ultimate purpose of affording creatures a duly proportioned participation in the divine life.[13]

The Son—the Father's eternally begotten Word we believe, or His ''formulative,'' ''definitive'' Image—''devises'' the structures or forms that constitute the created means, it seems, furthering the said plan's actual advancement. This complementing contribution involves ''elucidating'' the varied constitutent, generic and specific, essential patterns controlling creaturely existence. The Son-Word's ''consolidating,'' creative-redemptive role accordingly could correctly be called an ''organizing'' one, as distinguished from the Father's ''orienting,'' guiding counterpart. That truth presumably prompted Saint Paul's comment concerning Christ's profound personal import: ''In him everything . . . was created . . . all were created through him and for him. . . . In him everything continues in being.''[14]

Both the Old and the New Testament witness to the Holy Spirit's divine ''moving'' power. By image and impact, we learn of the third Person's characteristic creative-redemptive responsibility—''fomenting'' the governing plan's completion, or ''supplying and sustaining'' creatures' fundamental practical capacities. Exercising those finer, functional traits, the diverse creaturely types develop, proceeding toward their destined goals. The thus inherently given, dynamic inclinations represent relevant essential methods fostering the subject species' adequate enhancement (evolution), individually and collectively. In the ''mighty wind . . . over the waters'' at creation, and the ''driving wind . . . heard through the house'' at Pentecost, we see the Holy Spirit's peculiar invigorating power suitably symbolized.[15] One could consequently aptly identify the third Person with an ''operating'' role for the divine dynamism—translating the Father's and the Son-Word's relatively internal, ''directive'' and ''definitive'' determinations respectively, into external ''descriptive'' expressions.

The foregoing fundamental observations regarding the ''economic'' attributes of the three divine Persons indicate that they exert a basic overall ordering and undergirding vital influence on finite contingent beings. This theological truth (at least partly supernaturally revealed) is ontologically reflected, as extended, through the latters' common dynamic outlines, even though the seried balance between their central components differentiates them generically and specifically (by natures). We inevitably consider, implicitly anyway, these crucial controlling developmental vectors whenever conducting an investigation along standard scientific lines. A so penetrating observer then seeks systematic answers either proximately or remotely reflecting the inescapable objective factors noted earlier—''why,'' ''what,'' ''how.'' Stated more explicitly, the search entails efforts at understanding by correlating ends, means, and methods—or purposes, structures, and procedures, as historically-existentially modified. Each existing entity can be recognized, and reasonably classified, in a greater or lesser degree, according to its position on such an essentially proportionate scale. Since the typical qualities pertinent here are mainly substantial or spiritual, creatures' accompanying supplemental or corporeal features necessitate additional detailed categorical distinctions.

''The seried balance between central components'' mentioned above as differentiating creation dynamically (hence constitutionally too) derives from an especially close finite essential-existential connection with one of the divine Persons. This is so although every contingent being exhibits a similar relationship toward the other two Persons simultaneously. The critical distinguishing factor apparently represents a certain contrasting ''priority'' or ''prominence'' in creative responsibility for the respective types projected, which the several Persons characteristically exercise. Thus, the Son-Word's mediate Trinitarian status ''immanently''—actively ''consolidating'' the Father's ''conceptions'' and the Holy Spirit's ''completions,'' manifests itself ''economically'' through His peculiarly intimate impact upon human nature. The prominently blended, or sharply balanced, dynamic capacities essentially prevailing there (idealistic-theoretical and pragmatic-practical) remotely resemble the Son-Word's divine ''organizing'' contributions. They likewise make humanity the middle generic creaturely group. Combining angelical (idealistic-theoretical) and physical-biological (pragmatic-practical) created talents, it ''closes the gap'' dividing those radically disparate (yet mutually complementary) cosmic genera.[16]

Comprising creation's ''middle class,'' humans fill a mediating role aiding advancement of the divine creative-redemptive plan. They have been authorized and empowered to dominate physical-biological beings, but under angelic agents' direction (or consonant with divinely given and guiding norms).[17] Their providentially assigned cosmic position consequently carries a crucial salvific significance. When the eternally allotted time for God's preeminently personal intervention in the world's dynamic processes occurred, such a soul-shaking, social-sundering disclosure accordingly was most fittingly, if disarmingly, made through the Son-Word directly. The divine Mediator then assumed the created nature (human) that best reflects His immanent Trinitarian state, hence also best facilitates the Trinity's total (creative and redemptive) integral ''economic'' activity. That ''second-stage'' start of the Creator-creature relationship, whereby the latter were afforded access to an eternally abundant life, entailed certain necessary obligations on humanity's part. This latest, truly liberating—as descendentally enlightened (from above) opportunity involved identification with Christ—"the way, the truth, and the life." Since it required consistently close connections between the responding persons—really emulating the Trinitarian example, He inaugurated a similarly structured community (the Church). Under the Trinity's continuing guiding and guarding personal influence, its members labor at extending His saving mission (promoting the heavenly kingdom) world-wide.

Considering the critical importance of Christ's mediating role as the Father's divine Son-Word, the principal impact thereof upon His human condition is very pertinent for us. Carefully noting such connections, we can understand better what He meant when describing Himself as "the way, the truth, and the life." That effort hopefully will have an added helpful effect—providing telling vital lines linking these theological observations and the subsequent sociological conclusions. Foremost among His typical filial traits surely was the absolute obedience shown toward the Father's will. He regularly reiterated this obligation's overriding impress on His various earthly endeavors, as on His coming. It actually constituted "food" for Him.[18] The controlling purpose directing the messianic mission concerned abundant or eternal life, which He ultimately offered. Such enduring vitality really reflects the essential relationship between Father and Son-Word, originating with the first divine Person, yet eternally received and equally shared by the second divine Person. A duly proportionate, proximate participation in the latter glorifying state consequently comprises the final goal or end promised humans through Christ's message.[19]

Fulfilling the Father's will (purpose) governing the divine creative-redemptive plan implies corresponding complementary contributions from the Son-Word. As we recognized earlier, the Son-Word "elucidates" the created forms or structures befitting the end envisioned. Those generic-specific patterns represent the critically relevant means suitably insuring attainment of the assigned goals. At the human level, these essential constituents project a rather radically consolidated creature. This profoundly composite type combines spiritual and corporeal components, closely, as integrally, correlated; and demands decisive balancing endeavors (self-control) on the so personalized individual's part. A generic disorder prevailing there, engendered by an original existential defection (corporeal subverting spiritual), occasioned the Son-Word's subsequent personal incarnation. The truth regarding the chief corrective required to reestablish humanity's integrity, thus assuring eternal vitality, accordingly constituted His mission's central theme. Nothing less than a thorough reformation—a veritable rebirth, with spirit fully dominating flesh, can accomplish that saving result.[20] Such is the crucial meaning of the middle term in Christ's mediating message. It actually accentuates His own most characteristic, mediative, creative-redemptive impact upon human nature, as the Trinity's second divine Person.

We know very well how means only move toward intended ends through attendant methods. We also have seen above how the Holy Spirit provides this completing functional or operating power for the Trinity's divine dynamism—immanently and "economically" (creatively-redemptively). Christ clearly and convincingly manifested the Holy Spirit's personal presence within Him by the authoritive and auspicious actions He performed—preaching, teaching, healing, raising the dead, enduring the passion, finally His Resurrection and glorification. It was evidenced too, along somewhat more subdued lines, by the suffering servant role He portrayed. Both courses exemplify the "way" leading to the Father's given goal of eternal life, under human nature's fallen condition. Such a self-sacrificing, other-serving, saving path cannot be followed, however, unless the Holy Spirit inhabits and impels an individual or group. Similarly, the latter cannot receive the Former, unless they have already accepted and initially adopted the critical reforming attitude aligning them with the Son-Word. When thus reordered (reorganized), as were the first disciples from Christ's truth-conveying influence, the covertly enlightened neophytes are readied for the Holy Spirit's overtly "operating" or witnessing support. They then grow as they steadily go that way in the truth of life.[21]

Christ's mediating message and mission therefore conforms to the fundamental three-dimensional dynamism essentially controlling human, like all creaturely, existence. This elementary "energizing" order remotely reflects or refracts the immanent and "economic" activity characterizing the triune God-Creator. That "natural" connection between divinity and humanity has been both reaffirmed and readjusted (released from a deadly debilitating infirmity caused by human perversity) through Christ's redeeming efforts. Although His salvific import impinges first upon basic personal relationships, its total implications and ramifications actually extend much further. Obviously other innately modifying human features profoundly affect each one's development. Those chiefly include the categorically distinguishing or generically specifying qualities we classify as sexual, racial, and societal. They represent additional enrichening effusions, essentially, of the divinely devised structural pattern for human existence. This being so, we recognize them as primarily stemming from the Son-Word's distinctive "formalizing" creative contributions, albeit with the Father's accompanying "finalizing," and the Spirit's "functionalizing" aid. His incarnate redemptive impact consequently must have a similarly enlightening, reforming effect there too. In these respects, we will concentrate hereafter mainly on the mediating message's special societal significance.

NOTES

1. C. G. Jung, "The Relations between the Ego and the Unconscious," H. G. and C. F. Baynes, trans. in *The Basic Writings of C. G. Jung,* V. S. De Laszlo, ed. (New York: Random House, 1959), p. 154. C. G. Jung, "Psy-

chology and Religion: West and East,'' R. F. C. Hull, trans. in De Laszlo, *Basic Writings,* pp. 503–504. S. Freud, "The Ego and the Id," J. Riviere, trans. in *Complete Psychological Works of Sigmund Freud,* Standard Edition, Vol. 19, J. Strachey, ed. (London: Hogarth Press, 1961), pp. 24–27.

2. C. G. Jung. "The Structure and Dynamics of the Psyche," R. F. C. Hull, trans. in De Laszlo, *Basic Writings,* pp. 51–54. Jung, "Psychology and Religion," pp. 510–511. Freud, "The Ego and the Id," pp. 36–37.

3. Jung, "Relations between the Ego and the Unconscious," pp. 147–48. C. G. Jung, "The Psychology of Individuation," H. G. Baynes, trans. in De Laszlo, pp. 246–247. Freud, "The Ego and the Id," p. 25.

4. K. Rahner, "Guilt," *Theological Investigations* II (Baltimore: Helicon, 1963), pp. 272–73.

5. "In all creatures there is found the trace of the Trinity, inasmuch as in every creature are found some things which are necessarily reduced to the divine Persons as to their cause . . . as it is a created substance, it represents the cause and principle; and so . . . it shows the Person of the Father, Who is the principle from no principle. According as it has a form and species, it represents the Word, as the form of the thing made by art is from the conception of the craftsman. According as it has relation of order, it represents the Holy Spirit, inasmuch as He is love, because the order of the effect to something else is from the will of the Creator."—Thomas Aquinas, *Summa Theologica,* Part I, Q.45, A.7., Fathers of English Dominican Province, trans. (New York: Benziger, 1947), p. 238. (Vol. I). Reprinted by permission of Benziger Publishing Company.

6. Aquinas, *Summa Theologica,* Part I, Q.40, A.2, pp. 204–205. K. Rahner, *The Trinity,* J. Donceel, trans. (New York: Herder, 1970), pp. 98, 116–117.

7. Rahner, *The Trinity,* pp. 72–73.

8. Ibid., p. 75, note 29.

9. Ibid., p. 77.

10. M. J. Scheeben, *The Mysteries of Christianity,* C. Vollert, trans. (St. Louis: Herder, 1946), p. 138.

11. K. Rahner, *Nature and Grace,* D. Livingstone and G. R. Dimler, trans. (London: Sheed and Ward, 1963), pp. 125–126. Cf. Rahner, *Foundations of Christian Faith,* pp. 135–37.

12. Ephes. 1:4–9.

13. Ibid., verse 10.

14. Col. 1:16–17. Cf. Aquinas, *Summa Theologica,* Part III, Q.23, A.3; A.2, ad.3, pp. 2148–2149.

15. Gen. 1:2; Acts 2:2. "The energy of the divine life surges and culminates in the Holy Spirit . . . hence the communication of it to creatures must be . . . characterized as a communication of the Holy Spirit. . . ."—Scheeben, *Mysteries,* p. 393.

16. "Since all creation, both spiritual and corporeal, is represented in

man, God's supernatural mysterious cosmic plan is centered in man, not in the angels.''—Scheeben, *Mysteries,* p. 357; ''. . . Human nature . . . assumes in the universe a double position analogous to that of the Son . . . in the divinity. . . .''—Ibid., p. 362. Cf. Rahner, *The Trinity,* p. 90.

17. L. Boros, *Angels and Men* (New York: Seabury, 1976), p. 41ff.

18. John 4:33.

19. Ibid., 5:24–27; 6:57.

20. Ibid.; John 3:3, 35, 36; 8: 31–32; Rom. 3:25—Christ as ''means of expiation.'' Cf. Col. 1:20–Christ as ''means of reconciliation.''

21. Ibid., 14: 15–17, 26; 15: 26–27; 16: 13–15. Cf. ''The Church as Subject of the Sending of the Spirit,'' K. Rahner, *Theological Investigations VII* (New York: Herder, 1971), pp. 188–189.

Chapter Eight

CHRISTIAN REVELATION'S
SOCIETAL IMPORT

Parsons has shown how society's principal proximate components display a three-dimensional dynamism. The "polity" or political engagement provides a purposeful or goal defining societal service. Cultural and familial units supply what he terms "pattern-maintenance" facilities, although along notably different lines. Economic enterprises afford the tangible instruments and technical procedures needed to exploit productively society's physical-biological environment.[1] We likewise have seen that Sorokin and MacIver largely agree with Parsons on such crucial collective designations.[2] They do not go as far as the latter, however, in correlating closely the societal and personal aspects of the fundamental human dynamic.

Berger's looser, much more abstract, hence rather semi-angelic approach transcends those specifying social distinctions. His concern is twofold: expounding a socio-epistemological (philosophical) theory, and explaining the modifying import that historical factors hold for it.[3] Thus freed from complicating mediating formal societal features, he can speculate conveniently about the contrapuntal or competing contacts transpiring between these elemental extremities. No wonder he thinks there are "rumors of angels" around us, being so turned toward their trans-

98

mitting ''beam'' unknowingly. We noted earlier how this simplified stance makes him less a dissembler than his colleagues criticized here. Because he then has clearer vision, though, at that para-angelic level (little social ''dust'' beclouds it), his obtuse references to supernatural truth mark him as one whose own self-desire befogs it. Berger accordingly risks being counted among the direct defaulters, who actually prefer ''darkness'' while supposedly seeking the light. Self-determined, chiefly corporeally or sensibly convincing, plausibility alone satisfies him.

The crucial mistake made by such modernistically enlightened scientists reflects a profoundly personal (individually and societally) formal disorder. All four fail to recognize and respect human nature's consolidated structural condition (spiritual-corporeal) as a really relevant vital component certainly. An extravagantly natural, or secularistically subverted faith (ideology) leaves them laboring at interpreting collective relationships (cognitive and affective) in radical psychological darkness. Resembling the proverbial predicament—where blind men examine an elephant—these cognitively autonomous but affectively subjugated social analysts are rigidly restricted, hence ridiculously constricted, through their bodily bound beliefs. The resulting artifically, as superficially constructed theories they offer consequently represent technically or sensibly integrated, yet substantially enervated, ''professionally'' plausible concoctions. It's the ages-old (historically-pragmatically), self-deluding (philosophically-theoretically), drama reenacted in a contemporary, and ever more contemptible, setting. Emulating Kant, and his earlier, as also later-day, romantically ''free-thinking'' fellow-travellers, the said, allegedly serious, would-be human ''liberators'' actually evidence the truly enslaving effects attendant upon the cunning rationalistic processes they perpetrate. Having ''eaten the apple'' of invincible independence, thus insuring subjective dominion over objective reality, such subverted scientists dutifully rationalize (with ''professionally'' cultivated acumen) deep-set, demanding desires. They therefore exemplify, jointly and severally, the readily recognizable, self-enlightened expert—who "knows more and more about less and less." Here is "inflation" personified, befitting its supercilious, modernistic, mainly materialistic meaning, both as regards "higher standards" and "higher costs" of living.

The Christian revelation, authentically accepted and applied, banishes this corporeally confined, comfortably contrived, insidious subjugation. It does that principally by putting life's tempting tangible trappings in their proper place—supplemental to substantial-spiritual vital vlues. The so lifting (not simply loosening), liberating, radically reformed (really "reborn") state derives from a firmly founded supernatural faith. Such faith means believing the ample, integral testimony, subjectively-personally and objectively-societally given (implicit naturally, explicit supernaturally culminating with Christ), concerning a divinely decreed spiritual order intrinsically controlling reality.

Consequent upon the said faith's corresponding wisdom (supernatural sapientia)—its intellectual insight into the divine life-giving purpose—there follows consolidating knowledge (supernatural scientia) and its affective counterpart—hope—regarding the means available for advancing the said purpose. Then comes completing supernatural counsel regulating charity, or apt methods facilitating total fruition. As these chiefly cognitive-affective personal resources are mutually integrally activated (through humans' most tyical, mediating, formal reasoning faculties), amid their natural and increasingly supernaturalized environment —subjectively-personally and objectively-societally, they accomplish a proportionately perfecting development. The so truly (super-enlightened) believing, hoping, justly-charitably acting agents accordingly steadily move toward the predestined goal—eternal life.

Even when the freely offered supernatural vital assistance is avoided, either carelessly or defiantly, the same triple-tiered dynamism basically governs each subject's developmental process. Whatever the person's fundamental faith (affective attitude) with its accompanying foundational cognitive assumptions (wisdom), his or her ensuing hope-knowledge (reasoned evaluations) and extending charity-justice-counsel (practical applications) all stem from the underlying, conscious or unconscious, given beliefs. Very different comparative results accrue here however. If the faith is mainly natural, its overall effects inevitably entail a seriously stunted—spiritually subverted, corporeally perverted, "personal" and "societal" existence (the worldly wise plausible way). History copiously testifies to human nature's traditional disorderly tendencies, on an ever more "sophisticated" scale. The cleverly compromised naturalists thus become disastrously entrapped in a self and secularly inflated, hence really substantially deflated, existence, despite the rationalistically cultivated refinements.

As explained earlier, the critically important characteristic of the Christian revelation, so far as its direct implications for the recipients are concerned, is a decisive emphasis upon humanity's combined spiritual and corporeal content, together with the former's rightful essential dominion over the latter. Such a properly proportioned formal balance most truly reflects the divine vital impress constituting and activating human beings. Besides so profoundly or personally (consciously and responsibly) participating in the divinity's infinite substantial-spiritual immensity, humans were seen as similarly essentially and limitedly sharing the triadic dynamism (active relations) that concomitantly distinguishes the divine essence—concretely exemplified by the three perfectly equal Persons. Finite agents' essential developmental exigencies consequently refract the three divine Persons' respective, yet thoroughly concentrated, creative impact. Creatures therefore manifest the "Trinitarian traces" noted previously, through their final, formal, and functional causes (ends, means, methods), principally substantially-spiritually viewed. When considering humanity's crucial formal constitutent-core (spiritual-corporeal), we must understand correctly what that combination involves. To assist us here, we utilize additional theological contributions from Karl Rahner.

Rahner's study of symbolism is a very valuable and relevant aid. He titles this work "The Theology of the Symbol," and makes his analysis at three related levels: ontological, theological, and anthropological. Although we will focus mainly on the third, the first section provides some preliminary pointers thereto, as might well be expected. He opens, then, with the statement: ". . . the basic principle of an ontology of symbolism is as follows: all beings are by their nature symbolic, because they necessarily 'express' themselves in order to attain their own nature."[4]* Such a stand regarding the symbol requires a fundamental distinction: between "genuine symbols ('symbolic realities')" and "arbitrary 'signs,' 'signals,' and 'codes' ('symbolic representations')," he adds.[5] The first, primordial concept presently concerns us. It means, he says, a connection "in which one reality renders another present—primarily for itself, and only secondarily for others."[6] Not the representative relationship linking one object and another object, but the manifestation of an object's vital features through other immediately associated ones constitutes the symbolic condition we confront. Rahner explains the "symbolic reality" nexus as deriving from "the fact that all beings are multiple [in themselves], and are or can be the expression of another [or the self] in this plurality, by reason of [this] plural unity."[7]

Multiplicity or quantity shows clearly at the finite plane, obviously, in diverse parts and powers. That numerical characteristic is not merely a finite mark however, Rahner adds. It likewise reflects the Absolute Being as Trinity, though only dynamically or relationally, not constitutionally or substantially, the

*This and following excerpts from K. Rahner, *Theological Investigations IV*, K. Smyth, trans. (New York: Seabury, 1974) are reprinted by permission of the Winston Seabury Press.

case with finite contingent beings. Nevertheless, the creatures' unified self-realization by an expansion into plurality remotely resembles the divine plural unity ("Trinitarian traces"). "It is therefore true," Rahner affirms, "a being is, of itself, independently of any comparison with anything else, plural in its unity."[8]

Elucidating this plural unity theme further, he tells us,

> This means that each being, as a unity, possesses a plurality—implying perfection—formed by the special derivativeness of the plural from the original unity: the plural is in agreement with its source in a way which corresponds to its origin, and hence is "expression" of its origin by an agreement which it owes to its origin. Since this holds good for being in general, we may say that each being forms, in its own way, more or less perfectly according to its degree of being, something distinct from itself and yet one with itself, "for" its own fulfillment. . . . And this differentiated being, which is still originally one, is in agreement because derivative, and because derivatively in agreement is expressive.[9]

We therefore find the first statement ontologically justified, namely: "being is of itself symbolic, because it necessarily 'expresses' itself."

Rahner extends these explanations regarding "symbolic realities" (direct symbolism) to the psychological sphere, elementally anyway. Thus,

> The self-constitutive act whereby a being constitutes itself as a plurality which leads to its fulfillment . . . is however the condition of possibility of possession of self in knowledge and love . . . a being "comes to itself" in its expression, in the derivative agreement of the differentiated which is preserved as the perfection of the unity . . . it comes to itself in the measure in which it realizes itself by constituting a plurality . . . this means that each being—in as much as it has and realizes being—is itself primarily "symbolic." It expresses itself and possesses itself by doing so. It gives itself away from itself into the "other," and

there finds itself in knowledge and love, because it is by constituting the inward "other" that it comes to . . . its self-fulfillment,
which is the presupposition or the act of being present to itself
in knowledge and love.[10]

Such symbolism carries more than a self-knowing import, he
assures us. In real or objective knowing (understanding), "the
symbol is the reality in which *another* attains knowledge of a
being . . . the knowability and the actual knowledge of a being
(as object of knowledge) depend on the degree of actuality in the
thing to be known itself." Allowing for the knower's deficiencies,
"a being can be and is known, in so far as it is itself
ontically . . . symbolic. . . . The Being is known in this symbol . . . (else) it cannot be known."[11]

Turning back toward the ontological level again, we face
the problem of "how . . . the figure-forming essence of a
being . . . constitute[s] and perfect[s] itself." Rahner answers
the question as follows: "It does so by really projecting its visible
figure outside itself as its—symbol, its appearance, which allows
it to be there, which brings it out to existence in the world: and
in doing so, it retains it—'possessing itself in the other.' The
essence is there for itself and for others precisely through its
appearance—in the analogous measure, of course, in which a
being is there for itself and for others according to its own measure
of being."[12]

At this point we are ready to consider the real or direct
symbolic relationship's principal proximate pertinence—its bearing upon the human constitution, or the connection between body
and soul. Rahner's statements here rather provide foundational
links with the traditional enlightenment concerning human nature
examined earlier. As a summary start, he says, "the body is the
symbol of the soul, in as much as it is formed as the self-realization of the soul, though it is not adequately this, and the soul
renders itself present and makes its 'appearance' in the body
which is distinct from it."[13]

This affirmation is founded on the classical Greek and Christian tradition that the soul constitutes the substantial form of the body; "which alone can guarantee the strict unity of man, and the real humanness of his body," he adds. Succinctly expounding such a perennially relevant theme,

> Man is not composed of a soul and a body, but of a soul and [prime matter]. And this matter is of itself the strictly potential substratum of the substantial self-realization of the [soul] which by imparting itself thus gives its reality to the passive possibility of [prime matter], so that anything that is act (and reality) in this potentiality is precisely the soul. It follows at once that what we call the body is nothing else than the actuality of the soul itself in the "other" of (prime matter), the "otherness" produced by the soul itself, and hence its expression and symbol in the very sense . . . given to the term symbolic reality.[14]

Viewing the thus formally consolidated human being adequately, then, we see how the substantial-spiritual vital component decidedly influences all the actions that these so integrally combined subjects perform. Their varied engagements always reflect a certain complementary balance regarding the respective spiritual and corporeal contributions. When correctly organized (superior ordering inferior), the relatively external, tangible and spatially confined, bodily constitutents are activated under the supervision—guidance and guardance or cognitively and affectively, of the profoundly internal, intangible as spatially transcendent, spiritual counterparts. In other words, the latters' intellectual faculty should control (principal-agent) the imaginative-sensitive organs at the upper (cognitive) vital level. Similarly, the spirit's volitional faculty should correspondingly dominate the vegetative-sensitive organs at the under (affective) vital level. Likewise, the mental (upper set) of resources—intellectual-imaginative-sensitive—rightly exercise an active priority over the virile (under set) volitional-vegetative-sensitive—("looking before leaping," as we say), to insure guided, really gainful results. Such soundly, duly proportionately integrated persons (constitutionally anyway) possess a truly human substantive status.

This fundamentally personalized condition is not something attained absolutely or abstractly (purely theoretically-philosophically), as it were, amid the countless changing circumstances (practically-historically) marking finite reality. Rather does it gradually accrue (where the essential exigencies are responsibly respected) in accordance with the threefold developmental dynamism—ends, means, methods, previously seen as crucially contributing toward human fulfillment. For effective personal progress, therefore, every human being must maintain (increasingly) the formal substantial balance outlined above, on each dynamic plane, subjectively-personally and objectively-societally.

The process consequently requires an aptly apportioned (as already indicated) alignment of upper and under, inner and outer faculties (properly contrastingly correlated), while activating the three expansive or energizing sectors respectively. Discerning and determining ends demands the most upper and inner control over under and outer capacities. Supplying and selecting means entails a relatively moderate so structured control. Applying appropriate methods involves the least decisive dominion by the said prior or superior powers.

Since the human societal order derives from its subjects' social nature—representing necessary systematized collective efforts to meet common needs—it naturally reflects their essential vital traits. Parsons' dynamic distinctions in what he terms the "social systems" surely evidence that fact. We observed earlier how he classifies society's political sphere ("polity") as the goal-determining one (societal ends). Its cultural and familial areas are credited with critical conservational or "pattern-maintenance" roles—jointly and severally. They mediate between the polity and the economy, providing the socially formed members (societal means). These further assist the former and the latter at adequately exploiting environmental instrumental resources (societal methods) that promote the common good. Through such concerted complementary contributions, all founded on human members, a "societal community"—national, provincial or local—is seen developing wholesomely.

Neither Parsons nor other similarly secularly bound sociological specialists recognize any direct significance for the societal dynamism in human nature's distinctive spiritual content. Indirectly some allowances are made along those suprasensible lines, of course, by attributing a special import to the religious impact upon society's moral standards. Because both factors—religious and moral—receive attention merely as additional cultural components, however, they carry only "cybernetic" (physical-biological) organizational value, like the remaining collective contrivances contained there. So chiefly corporeally construed, hence simply historically derived and applied (yet obviously possessing a mysterious psychological efficacy), their public legitimation follows from popular approval and more or less explicit political authorization. That general-interest agency's assertedly dominant legalizing responsibilities supposedly ultimately control overall societal relationships here as elsewhere. This sensibly slanted scientific interpretation accordingly implicitly affirms the religio-moral sector's mainly bodily impact, through thus subjugating it to temporal civil authority, as regards the relevance of society's normative needs.

The Christian revelation's tellingly spiritual thrust breaks the bodily bind constricting and restricting human development —individually-personally and collectively-societally. By removing the sensible "scales" blinding the naturally bound-down, secularly subdued "eyes," it opens the way for advancement toward a truly realistic or thoroughly abundant life. With a supernatural faith in Christ (and His personal-communal "symbolic reality"—the Church), founded upon reasonable objective evidence exposing and expanding the natural order's temporally and spatially transcendent connections, the proportionately enlightened believers increasingly see beyond their corporeal confines. To the extent they do, the latter's vital prominence is correspondingly surpassed, dwindling before the spirit's preeminent powers. The resultant, radically revised ("reborn") condition, rather than denying the body's worth altogether, actually enhances it (then envisioned as symbolizing and consequently sharing a supernatural status).

Such an intensely improved (freed from enervating excesses), substantially integrated state properly prevails on both the personal and societal planes. Besides fostering a progressively permanant fulfillment in society's personalized subjects, it similarly facilitates solid improvements throughout the former's collective counterparts. These constitutional clarifications concomitantly promote more accurate conceptions and commitments concerning correct correlations between the social whole's (societal community) attendant and equally important dynamic divisions—ends, means, methods. Those most typical developmental units—political (purposeful), cultural-familial (structural), economic (procedural), secularly summarized, thereafter are seen as making their distinctive vital contributions (cognitively and affectively), principally along parallel but contrasting (spiritual and corporeal) interlocking lines. The secularized "substitious," one-dimensional substantive view is thus realistically expanded, likewise liberated, sociologically as well as psychologically. Our crucial controlling standard for distinguishing the spiritual and corporeal (inner and outer) essential constitutencies here, represents an extension of the same one applied at the personal level. It accordingly entails differentiating the aforenoted central-societal combinations exhibiting a decisively dominant influence by universalizing generic-specific (integrating) features prevailing over individualizing particular (separating) factors, from those manifesting a merely marginal dominion by the former over the latter, within each dynamic sector.

Following the basic systematic outline which Parsons has helpfully given us, while undertaking this supernaturally enlightened societal reappraisal, we focus first on the "polity" or political division. Designating its role as alone providing society's goal-determining or chief purposeful services reflects the "substitious" scientists' fundamental epistemological error—fallacy of misplaced concreteness. Although humans' bodily vitality naturally displays a certain spiritual impress immediately, through unified parts and powers, consistent reinforcing assistance from the spirit's own profound discerning and determining capacities is required for trully progressive activity (as Rahner explained earlier). Otherwise the body rather resembles the proverbial "bull in a china shop," reacting to restrictive surroundings. Actually it can never be entirely free of that additional spiritual impact, considering their essential formal connection. The body's "bipartisan" import may become excessive, however, as happens when the spirit allows corporeal concerns a disproportionate preference. Then we have the subverted, "substitious" human condition, whether crudely or cleverly contrived. Permitting the "polity" or political societal agency's claim upon dominant directive or goal-determining authority represents the said personal distortion immensely enlarged.

Since both a person's and a group's purpose (end) basically, even if unconsciously, affects accompanying dynamic facilities (means, methods) correspondingly, such preeminence afforded the "polity" inevitably causes pronounced politicizing effects in the societal community's overall dynamism. Civil-legal values and norms ordinarily are automatically identified with the spiritual-moral kind (so far as the latter receive official attention), the religious aspects thereof being relegated to the private, cultural sector. We observed earlier how this has traditionally characterized the native Oriental and African religio-ethical customs. We likewise examined still more extensively the Occidental peoples' deliberate downward drift toward the same primitive politicized societal life (technologically disguised), from which the Christian revelation's social ramifications had previously raised them. Correctly supernaturally viewed (spiritually and corporeally), the "polity" or political institution (State) appropriately exercises only tangible temporal corporeal purposeful guidance on the societal community's behalf, as befits the chiefly bodily competence it possesses. Society's spiritual-moral direction regarding goals is properly supplied by its religious agencies, and mainly the Christian Church.

Aptly conceived and similarly overtly construed, the Church constitutes the perennial communal presence of Christ—the ultimate supernatural revelatory source for humanity. In that universally responsible role, the Church authoritatively defines and declares—principally through divinely commissioned and conserved officials—the spiritual values and moral norms insuring humans' (personally and collectively) adequate orientation (eternal life). Though really a distinct societal "faculty" alongside the political "organ," it cannot rightly be viewed as separate from the latter. Such a subjectively and "substitiously" concocted interpretation reflects the modernistically "enlightened" effort to "bury" the spirit beneath the body secretly, while ostensibly pseudoscientifically "liberating" both. The Church therefore provides the "polity" (State) with temporally transcendent assistance, whereby this secular authority can propound and enforce distinct civil-legal values and norms having a sound spiritual-moral basis. The relationship thus involves mutually complementary contributions between superior and inferior (like spirit and body) societal components. Consequently, the Church is not simply a humanly devised cultural phenomenon, but a divinely given goal-determining religious entity, affording society supremely fulfilling aid. It is the primary or major symbol of the abiding supernatural revelation.[15]

Tragically, the Church's communal unity has been damaged badly by large-scale serious divisions. Humans' inveterate independent inclinations—inherently justifiable on the corporeal plane considering matter's intrinsic particularizing traits—have breached their natural boundaries, however, here as elsewhere. The separatist tendency has invaded the spiritual realm intensifying these compromising creatures' "substitious" bent (artifically cultivated) enormously. Autonomous approaches to the original Christian revelation spawned similar rebellious attitudes toward its original communal institution. Our initial reflections concerning the adverse scientific-philosophic ramifications stemming from Luther's religious revolt implicitly indicate the corresponding harm done against the Church directly. That pluralizing (even plagiarizing) of the traditional community "paved the way" for the proportionately exaggerated emphasis upon reality's quantitive, corporeal or sensible, features characterizing modernistic secularistic "enlightenment." Together they increasingly depict the pluralism-syndrome's "sophisticated" absurdity, which, as we saw before, advocates (consciously or not) a fantastically fragmatic ideal of human fulfillment, knowing and doing more and more (quantitively-sensibly) about less and less (qualitively-spiritually).

The Church organically instituted and commissioned by Christ (rather than the countless fundamentalistic and pseudo-sophisticated individualistic cryptotypes) is still in society's midst. It persists at proffering and promoting the supernaturally revealed way, truth, and life, overcoming the bodily bound darkness enthralling humanity. It can be recognized through the continuing conflict experienced with the worldly wise proponents of secularly subverted plausibility, while holding up the Cross as the spiritually controlling moral path alone insuring real integrity.

Those who oppose this "straight and narrow" course—not simply elementally but really comprehensively or on overall balance adequately viewed, either overtly or cleverly covertly—are well symbolized by the ever-ready (and heady, popularly plausible) enthusiasts for change. They largely incarnate another admonition that Christ issued: ". . . wide is the way leading to destruction, and great the number traveling it. . . ."[16]

NOTES

1. Parsons, *Social Systems,* p. 192–196, 201, 254–255.
2. Sorokin, *Society,* chapters 11 and 12. MacIver, *Society,* chapters 11, 18, 19, 20.
3. Berger, *Social Construction,* Introduction, p. 51–52, 92–128, 181–182.
4. K. Rahner, "The Theology of the Symbol," *Theological Investigations* IV, trans. K. Smyth (New York: Seabury, 1974), p. 224.
5. Ibid., p. 225.
6. Ibid.
7. Ibid., p. 225–226.
8. Ibid., p. 227.
9. Ibid., p. 228.
10. Ibid., pp. 229–230.
11. Ibid., pp. 230–231.
12. Ibid., p. 231.
13. Ibid., p. 247.
14. Ibid.
15. *Constitution on the Church in the Modern World,* 2nd Vatican Council, nn. 40, 76. Cf. Schillebeeck, *Christ, the Sacrament,* pp. 201–202. J. Maritain, *Integral Humanism,* J. W. Evans, trans. (New York: Scribner's, 1968) pp. 291–297.
16. Matt. 7:13–14.

Part IV

Chapter Nine

SOCIETY'S CRUCIAL SPIRITUAL-CORPOREAL CORRELATIONS

Before pursuing our societal analysis further along these distinct, not separate, essential constitutional lines, it appears advisable to consider the implications thereof somewhat more closely. Such additional clarification should help in understanding better the distinctions drawn not only at society's purposeful or goal-determining level, but as regards the other dynamic divisions (means and methods) also. Affirming the Church's authentic spiritual-moral guiding societal role does not indicate its purely spiritual status. We noted earlier how human nature combines spirit and matter on an intimately integrated scale. The single substantial spiritual principle concertedly activates the accompanying material component differentially. When the former does this with a bare preponderance of unifying influence over the latter's contrasting centrifugal tendencies, we have humans' corporeal, sensitive-vegetative manifestations (physical-biological organism). When the spirit exercises that centralizing (generic-specific) impact upon the bodily organs' particularizing traits more or less comprehensively, hence properly predominantly, we have humans' spiritual, sensibly transcendent capacities (cognitive-affective) evidenced. The difference, then, is between an inferior, temporal, earthbound outlook and output, in relation to a superior, eternally elevated, and tangibly liberated (proportionately, not absolutely) one.[1]

A certain spiritual and material balance accordingly holds at each dynamic vital level. If the counterparts' connection entails a close correlation, a correspondingly corporeal (temporal-spatial) condition prevails. If the said constitutive linkage displays a decided disparity, emphasizing more profoundly personal processes, a supraspatial-temporal or spiritual state perdures. These crucial formal human distinctions are most clearly recognized comprehensively, and, where rightly respected, similarly completely developed, chiefly through our organic communal relationships.[2] Such aptly self-transcending commitments, with attendant increased personalizing consequences, will not be attainable regularly and really responsibly, however, unless the interacting subjects receive adequate enlightening and empowering help from supernatural revelation. Lacking this reforming aid, those naturally warped (individualistically unbalanced) agents mainly incline toward either a sensibly subverted "substitious" stance openly, or surreptitiously under a superstitious cover. Our previous investigations concerning the traditional Oriental (Mongoloid) and African (Negroid) religio-ethical practices, and the modernistically "enlightened" Occidental (Caucasoid) pseudomorality, surely have demonstrated these facts of life.

The Christian Church supplies the supernatural spiritual-moral assistance that the societal community (local, regional, national, and international) needs for virile health. When that invigorating contribution is accepted and applied by the "polity" (State) to its own proper civil-legal involvements, those heavily tangibly and temporally weighted, relatively corporeal engagements have a fuller human value. They are then blended better, spiritually and materially. Conversely, since the Church still has natural features, prominently corporeal, while existing on earth, it rightly respects the "polity's" valid directions regarding their use as affecting the common temporal good. A mutually complementary connection should persist here accordingly, befitting the deference due between the human spirit and body.[3] Obviously, such a correct balance in society's "goal-determining" sector has experienced a serious setback from the multiple divisions scandalously marring the Church. The excessive pluralistic ramifications thereof cannot be entirely avoided. Nonetheless, although prime responsibility for removing this disgraceful defect rests principally with the ecclesial community, the "polity" is not meanwhile entitled to employ the spiritual "split" as a defense against any association (complete separation). That "sophisticated" self-righteous stand only fosters its own frustration—secular subversion. The truly human or reasonable (spiritually-corporeally integrated) attitude would encourage efforts at reunion, indirectly certainly, like utilizing joint advisory services by the somewhat more organized denominations.

Establishing societal goals and promoting their achievement clearly entail different endeavors. Additional action must be taken toward linking them with the means and methods capable of advancing those purposes. Consequently, on the tangible-temporal, civil-legal communal plane, the "polity" properly propounds and enforces pertinent norms (also affords stimulating aids) along these overall unifying lines. In doing so, though, it responsibly exercises restraint, leaving appropriate openings for the other collective types' valid autonomy. A similar extended relationship holds at the spiritual-eternal religio-moral level, where the Church justifiably issues relevant guidelines (also provides practical assistance) facilitating a higher and deeper societal unity amid an authentically autonomous dynamic diversity.[4] Lacking such wholesome systemization, a society steadily deteriorates into a massive mess—corporeal bulk or quantitive power cloaking a spiritual hulk or qualitive void—howsoever artfully articulated. The disguise may assume a banal (yet lethal) bluff, as among aggressively atheistic ideologic communities; or it may adopt a glamorous, generous appearance (killing through "kindness"), as with the romantically secularistic sort.

Refocussing our attention upon the societal community's cultural and familial realms, which Parsons has termed "pattern maintenance" components, we note again how this critical stabilizing status really makes them the chief collective means sustaining the total social entity. Their characteristic consolidating contributions—propagating, preliminary training (by the family), and educating, advanced training (by cultural agencies), mainly form the membership for suitable roles in society. They thus provide key mediating linkage between the general purposeful, "goal-determining," religious and political services, and the correspondingly common, relatively procedural benefits forthcoming from economic enterprises. As on the preceding purposeful plane, spiritual and corporeal vital distinctions must be recognized and respected here too. The familial institution's strong physical-biological ties give it a decidedly corporeal bent, within the essential limits explained above. Contrastingly, the cultural combine's predominantly intellectual-volitional connections carry a proportionate spiritual emphasis. Correctly constituted and reciprocally correlated, then, they exemplify human nature's mediate or means dynamism in its most comprehensive personal or communal living aspects.[5]

Both the Church and the "polity" (State) supply important coordinating assistance (spiritual-moral and civil-legal guidelines respectively) for these middle level societal divisions. They also provide valuable practical services. This helps "repay," as it were, the complementary organizing, formational aid that the latter naturally affords. When so rightly, supernaturally-naturally aligned, each "pattern maintenance" sector exercises an authentic autonomy while seeking proper development. When not so soundly integrated, more often than not the modern collective condition, radically revised relationships ensue. Cultural and familial units may join with the Church's struggle against a perverse domination by the "polity"—the situation under so-called collectivism, really disguised group-egoism (the Party). Somewhat less concertedly, a minority of cultural and familial entities follow the Church's lead in combatting a pluralistically secularized or compromised societal attitude (individualism, likewise disguised as groups) prevailing among the majority.

As we saw before, Parsons assigns society's economic dynamic sector a comparatively dominant procedural role. It produces the tangible goods and services, representing the principal instrumental means and technical methods, facilitating the other communal organs' apt advancement. He recognizes the fundamental fact that each collective agency necessarily performs some operations along those rather detailed expansive lines. Relative to the societal community's functional needs as a whole, though, the economic enterprises' contributions are credited with more general relevance. We may advisedly recall here our earlier observations regarding the interrelatedness marking distinctions between such critical dynamic categories (personally and communally). Since they reflect human nature's share in the divine Trinitarian personal dynamism, they accordingly manifest "overlapping" aspects of the intricate intimacy amid decisive difference characterizing the divine relationships.

Given humanity's consolidated constitution (spiritual-corporeal) also, the contrary yet complementary consequences stemming therefrom must be considered too, at this economic dynamic level. Society has definitely distinguishable essential traits, then, on the mainly procedural or overall methodical plane, as was seen the case on the contrasting purposeful or ends' and structural or means' strata. Thus, we properly distinguish the economy's fine arts (goods and services for spiritual development), and its mundane arts (goods and services satisfying corporeal needs).[6] These variations in vital form economically, due to humans' essentially blended content, remain consistent with those previously found regulating the religious-political and the cultural-familial connections. They therefore promote similar mutually beneficial exchanges by way of further fostering a thoroughly wholesome communal condition.

As the products obtained through the said distinctive economic sources differ quite prominently, so do their organizational and operational modes (function follows form). While the working units comprising both realms rightly enjoy an appropriate autonomy, greater independence naturally is allowed the fine arts. That necessarily follows from the transcendent spiritual qualities especially impregnating the latter. Nonetheless, because both share human nature's dual constitutional correlations (spiritual-corporeal), proportionality, they are respectively subject to the Church's spiritual-moral and the ''polity's'' civil-legal, guiding or purposeful directives, correspondingly balanced.[7] These economic agencies receive important practical help here too. They likewise are influenced significantly by the intervening or mediating cultural-familial formational contributions, as already noted, and vice versa of course.

Unless economic artistry responsibly adopts true moral norms, implementing supernatural-natural, spiritual-corporeal vital values, which the Church has either announced or approved, it experiences a perennial extravagant problem—obscenity. This serious disorder can occur also in the cultural-familial and even the religious-political realms, because human nature's ''scenic'' features—sensibly detailed or esthetic, mark those dynamic divisions too. Such scenarios chiefly characterize society's economic sector, however, especially fine arts (qualitatively) consonant with its eminently tangible practical emissions. That implies a more readily evident, though not always more humanly important, presence there. ''Scenic'' supplements to otherwise strongly theoretic situations (religiously, politically, culturally, familially) exert possibly less noticeable but profoundly penetrating influences, for good or ill. Visual and aural aids (sometimes tactile as well) usually have a potent impact upon human relationships at all levels. Still, identifying and confronting obscenity under the economy's largely open or publicly asserted conditions, should help better toward preventing or correcting it elsewhere; subject to the crucial cultural-familial formational roles.

The Christian revelation affords direct enlightening assistance here. After listing the principal perverse traits that emerge "from within a man [and] come from the deep recesses of the heart," Christ uncovers their crucial personal cause—"an obtuse spirit."[8] As the obtuse angle represents an overly loose use of the standard right angle geometrically, so the "obtuse spirit" overextends the morally tolerable balance between humanity's spiritual and corporeal components. The resultant sensibly subverted hence personally perverted, seriously false state reflects this obtuseness in its expressive details. Such a scenario is an obscenity: a radical derogation from the true justice and charity owed by the purveyors to themselves and to other societal members. Making decisions on that artistic score obviously requires clear conceptions concerning human nature's ultimate purposeful, structural, and procedural capacities. The Church supplies those controlling spiritual-moral guidelines, advisedly aided there through consultative contacts with pertinently experienced and responsible, economic (also cultural-familial) professionals. It likewise should receive due civil-legal support as the "polity" (State) finds appropriate.

ULTIMATE THEOLOGICAL-SOCIOLOGICAL CONCLUSIONS

The foregoing considerations regarding the Christian revelation's more proximate societal import prepare us for some ultimate theological conclusions. These involve interpreting the fundamental vital impact of Christ's mediating creative role, as the Son-Word or second divine Person, upon human society's most typical integral features. In this intriguing connection, we first recall Christ's statement summarizing His redemptive mission—"I am the way, the truth, and the life. . . ." Then we recall our earlier investigations into that epic announcement's basic interpersonal implications anent the Trinity. We have seen how it concisely indicates the infinite dynamism linking Himself (the Son-Word) and the other two divine Persons (the Father and the Holy Spirit). Each act He performs, whether strictly tri-personal (immanent-Trinity), or concomitantly creational ("economic"-Trinity), bespeaks such perfect integrity. His actions accordingly always occur on what could correctly be termed a triple-aligned scale—deference to the Father, reference to Himself, and deference to the Holy Spirit. Thus does He fulfill the Son-Word's mediating role.

Envisioned somewhat more explicitly, or as additionally humanly exemplified, we may analogously interpret Christ's divine, dynamically distinct, yet substantially-spiritually equal, Trinitarian status along standard psychic (cognitive-affective) linking lines. He "formulates" the "consolidating," "theoretical-practical," insightful decisions that join, as it were, the Father's logically prior "inspiring theoretical conceptions" with the Holy Spirit's logically subsequent "practical applications." Those divine interpersonal relations therefore originate—as ultimate "orienting" (final), "organizing" (formal), and "operating" (functional) Principles respectively, the fundamental developmental dynamism (ends, means, methods) invigorating every creature. The latter essentially spiritual-substantial qualities (materially embodied), though maintaining their elemental vital priorities, differentiate creatures generically (implicitly specifically) by a proportionately arranged, proximate alternate emphasis among themselves. Humans consequently were seen as stressing especially the means-sector, because of a typically blended (spiritual-corporeal) or mediate constitutional condition (between the angelic and physical-biological genera). They do that while giving properly complementary attention to prior guiding ends and subsequent assisting methods. When so aptly ordered, they actually, albeit remotely, reflect the Son-Word's mediating role within the divine Trinity. The way, truth, and life He offers them as humanly incarnate in Jesus Christ insures an adequate emulation of His exemplarity, hence their thorough personal fulfillment, as imagining the Trinity's creative-redemptive import for humanity.

Two points made above should be clarified before proceeding further. The threefold features characterizing Christ's creative-redemptive role (way, truth, life) as Son-Word represent a unified, single activity. They reflect His free filial obedience toward the Father—life or "ends"-Source, His own responsible complementary contribution thereto—truth or "means"-Source, and His free communing with the Holy Spirit—way or "methods"-Source. He accordingly is personally involved mainly through the middle or mediate aspect, while sharing (giving and receiving) simultaneously through the other two. Thus human nature, principally created by Him, typically manifests that correlation, as already mentioned.

Secondly, we must view these various states of the divine vital dynamism against the absolute or total infiniteness that their pure spirituality includes. The existential power they possess has no conceivable limits (barring contradictions), even if acting under created material conditions. Although essentially finite, matter, because spiritually impregnated, participates in the latter's limitless being. This fundamental fact can be discerned from the countless numbers comprising the human genus, besides the innumerable physical-biological counterparts. Each member within the former category refracts the same, divinely given, constitutional core (spiritual-corporeal), more or less actively (giving and receiving) committed to a partially self-determined development, through a "triple-geared" vital dynamism. The said basic organic fact is evidenced still better by such qualitive features marking the myriad concrete subjects. On that principally dispositional or personal score, rather than the prior positional or individual one (largely anyway), the divinity's measureless immensity makes a yet greater self-disclosure.

Humanity's essential capacities cannot be expressed adequately if activated merely at the relatively individual level, howsoever numerous the agents. They require much sharper refinements to represent the Trinitarian qualitive impress upon them. For this reason, then, human nature's basic generic qualities are additionally differentiated, chiefly along standard dynamic lines, through innate class-characteristics (species). Those readily recognizable distinctions have been common classified as sexual, racial, and societal respectively. The second and third display multiple internal primal-typical variations not possessed by the first (like human nature itself). Each reflects an enrichening extension of humans' elemental share in the divine largess.

These enlivening expansions necessarily follow the "triple-tiered" arrangement integrating the fundamental human dynamism (ends, means, methods). Since the societal ramifications alone concern us here, it appears advisable to omit needless comments regarding the other two. While passing over closer comparisons, we should note that the societal strain, as the most advanced or comprehensive one, correspondingly has more numerous subsidiary groupings. We previously distinguished the former's major divisions, which stem from such extended vital infusions enhancing human nature. Discreetly constitutionally aligned, and similarly dynamically correlated, they are the religious-political, cultural-familial, and economic fine arts-mundane arts. They evidence humanity's essential societal exigencies, ends, means, and methods respectively, spiritually and corporeally considered. Viewed inversely and summarily, they comprise more thorough realizations of the way, the truth, and the life; or humans' crucial original, created connection with the Son-Word's mediating Trinitarian role.

His redemptive mission, humanly incarnate in Jesus Christ, entailed explicating exactly those essential vital components' meaning—cognitively and affectively (enlightened "from above" rather than "from below"). Realistically, He began this salvific effort by working on the recipients at the elemental or individual personal level. It is meant for all personal relationships, though, channelled chiefly through the generically typical sexual, racial, and societal species, under the Church's representative spiritual-moral suzerainty. As perfect personal mediator, Christ's messianic reformational course reaffirmed supernaturally the critical natural truth so pertinent to humanity's mediate creaturely status—the medium (form-means) is the message. Starting with a profound personal conversion—reasserting the spirit's rightful dominion over the body ("recombining" the form or means)—the saving, freeing ("the truth will set you free") process gradually permeates society, where responsibly respected.

Parsons was certainly correct in recognizing the central contribution of the "pattern maintenance" or cultural-familial (means-elucidating, formational) societal sector. Emulating his "scientifically enlightened" modernistic counterparts, however, he interpreted society's overall system leaving out its life-giving "leaven"—spirit, as a consciously controlling, not a subconsciously subverted constitutent. The results really reflect the qualitively flat, flabby, and flaccid existence so characteristic of contemporary social relations, despite their gaudy, giddy, sensibly slanted or fanciful facade. Christ came "that they may have life and have it to the full."[9] Such eternal life (personally and societally) is possible solely through the morally "straight and narrow" truth and way (means and methods) that He persistently provides. They elucidate the essential content of humanity's true common good. This requires a spiritual "rebirth"—cognitively and affectively—if we are to benefit from His personal presence: as Son-Word, humanly incarnate, mediating the Father's and the Holy Spirit's supernaturally invigorating divine influence, in and with His Church responsibly serving the whole societal community.

So far as the Church succeeds at that universal supernaturalizing task—aiding the common good's advancement by its apt moral-spiritual impact, amid each typical societal sector, on a worldwide scale, it promotes Christ's consummating goal. As He prayed: "that all may be one as you, Father, are in me, and I in you, that all may be one in us" (John 17:21). It likewise fulfills Saint Paul's eschatological ideal, or promoting human unity by "the knowledge of God's Son," so forming a perfected humanity that is "Christ come to full stature" (Eph. 4:12–13).

NOTES

1. Rahner, *Hearers of the Word*, pp. 55, 85–93; 129–141.
2. Ibid., pp. 133–134.
3. *Constitution on the Church in the Modern World*, Second Vatican Council, n. 76. Maritain, *Integral Humanism*, pp. 176–182.
4. Second Vatican Council, nn. 73–75.
5. Ibid., nn. 47–52; 57–62.
6. J. Messner, *Social Ethics*, J. J. Doherty, trans., rev. ed., (St. Louis and London: B. Herder, 1965), p. 752. Cf. J. Barzun, *The Use and Abuse of Art* (Princeton: University Press, 1974), p. 123. R. Nisbet, *Sociology as an Art Form* (New York: Oxford University Press, 1976), p. 10.
7. Second Vatican Council, nn. 63–64.
8. Mark 7:20–23.
9. John 10:10.

Chapter Ten

SOCIETY AS A REALITY

Another aspect of society's spiritual import should be considered. It concerns the collective enterprise's essential identity, whether that agency actually exists, or has merely a fictitious reality. Allowing for different degrees or shadings, two apparently drastic alternatives traditionally have been offered as answers. One admits only the latter artificial condition, claiming the resultant combination simply represents so many individual (pseudopersonal) relationships. The latter alone are real. Poles apart theoretically, another advocates the collectivity's supreme if not sole reality, individuals (supposed persons) being but massive components thereof.[1] Practically, though, as already indicated, this second view constitutes a cleverly disguised variation on the individualistic theme. It is the idealistic ideology, which, when overtly applied, becomes radical group-egoism or revolutionary romanticism. Since no whole can exist without distinctive constituents (even God manifests a Trinitarian existence), collectivism entails control by an allegedly omnipotent political clique, or glorified gangsterism. The relevant problem confronting us here accordingly involves determining if society possesses a certain factual reality, or rather reflects a fictional projection mythically interpreting individual interaction.

The modernistically enlightened sociologists, whose views

have been analyzed briefly above, evidence at least a latent inclination toward the openly individualistic (pseudopersonalistic) outlook. They hardly could avoid such an evolutionary romantic attitude, while faithfully following a Kantian liberated, acutely autonomous, slickly subjectivistic "constructionist" approach. Their passionate rationalism, founded upon a naturalistic faith, with its implicit professional elitism, necessarily aligns them against this atomistic, relatively opportunistic (laissez faire) societal stance, however. That comparatively primitive, crudely competitive social arrangement largely contradicts the intricately systematized traits that they arbitrarily, albeit articulately, attribute to society. Nevertheless, despite enterprising endeavors emphasizing the collective connections' reality, supposedly distinct from the individual contributions comprising it, the results achieved remain quite ambiguous. This uncertainty is inevitable and understandable, because the explanations proffered carry a dubious conviction, displaying the sensibly subverted authors' "substitious" or substitutional insights and interpretations. Thus, although arguing along somewhat objectively synthesized or realistically organic societal lines fundamentally and remotely, their more proximate and vitally meaningful elucidations convey a loosely, obtusely individualistic (pseudopersonalistic) impression.

1. Parsons apparently acknowledges society's immanent reality, as a living system.[2] Yet, given his sensible-empirical, consciously subjectivistic cognitive limitations, he interprets its observable order mainly in mechanistic, "cybernetic," built-in physical-biological, hence decidedly quantitive, chiefly corporeally or individualistically significant terms. For him, then, social systems are merely theoretical rationalizations of human beings' extensive, rather intensive, inherent gregarious inclinations. No objectively recognizable, essentially enduring, comprehensively self-controlling, substantive pattern or nature exerts a decisive dynamic influence here. Only more sophisticated elementary exigencies than the kind marking other objects around

them, characterize these artfully active agents.[3] They accordingly adopt conveniently contrived values and norms consonant with intrinsic evolutionary impulsions. Such institutionalizing outcome is determined by numerically prevailing testimony to plausibility. The ''complicatedness of a value-system . . . is clearly a function of the pluralism . . . of the social system,'' says Parsons. That pluralism includes many value patterns, and the multiple interests they aim at regulating. When pressure on the former becomes critical from polarization among the latter, pluralism still holds, he believes. ''In most cases it is intrinsically possible . . . that such polarizations should be resolved by redefining the relevant value-patterns on a level of sufficient generality to include both sides of the previous polarity.[4]

2. MacIver similarly takes a stand against both the individualistic (pseudopersonalistic) and the collectivistic attitudes toward society. Like Parsons, however, he actually accentuates the first type while explaining the societal relationship. As a ''web of relationships,'' it is ''a becoming, not a being; a process, not a product.''[5] Furthermore, those principally practical links are intended for ''the support of and contribution to the ends-purposes of individuals themselves,'' we learn. Since he stresses their autonomy—centers ''of activity and response expressive of a nature that is (their) own,'' no real qualitive problem regarding a counterbalancing common good bothers him.[6] The requisite integrating effort evidently carries a prominently quantitive import—promoting processes that facilitate individually inclined interactions. MacIver consequently rather echoes Parsons's fundamentalistic emphasis on abstract value-generalization as the prime regulatory factor insuring societal harmony. Its the old pluralistic adage—''doing it by the numbers,'' in effect. Because they believe essentials have simply elemental value (theoretical), practically interpreting and implementing them mainly entails achieving mutual subjective agreement among the pertinent individual participants, humanly speaking.

3. Sorokin apparently sees society possessing its own reality.

An individual's (pseudoperson) development is derived chiefly from his or her collective relationships, he tells us.[7] Also, we noted earlier his conviction that the social subject's personal peace depends upon the solidarity of such groups. Despite these fundamentally objective observations concerning societal existence, further strengthened by accepting the human mind's access to suprasensible empirical data, we find him displaying a somewhat strong individualistic (supposed personalistic) bias, implicitly anyway. Society is defined merely as the sum total of mutual relations.[8] Thus lacking basic connections with a correspondingly recognizable and commonly responsible, qualitively unifying component—like an essential common good—the said "totality" practically represents a loose quantitive individualistic conglomerate.

As stated bove, Sorokin discerns a close correlation between individual (pseudoperson) and societal development. Yet we previously saw how he "partitions" the "person" psychically into multiple egos, stemming from respective relevant collective engagements. Viewed the other way around, then, the groups spawning such supposed personal divisions must manifest a similar disparity among themselves. That reciprocal conclusion receives additional confirmation when measured against the practical ramifications of the foregoing existentially conglomerized ("totality") societal conception. The reasons for Sorokin's discontinuity, as regards theoretical intimations and practical interpretations, on the societal score, ultimately resemble those characterizing Parsons's and MacIver's positions. All three lack rational consistency, because they omit conscious attention to reality's (especially human) wholesomely vitalizing, as commonly yet distinctively constituted, objectively and subjectively oriented, substantial spiritual core. Their naturalistically enlightened, corporeally concentrated outlook actually identifies society's reality with its myriad individual (pseudopersonal) members, practically or existentially. The elegantly elaborate, elementally integrating essential explanations they offer largely reflect abstract, professionally plausible (numerically considered) theoretical constructions.

4. Berger says, "Society exists both as an objective and a subjective reality."[9] These complementary counterparts are dialectially related. Being another modernistic believing scientist, albeit lately showing some "revisionist tendencies," his concepts concerning reality in those two respects differ radically from traditional pre-Enlightenment notions. The latters' exponents see the first term (objective) including qualitive, substantial-durable, more or less common (generic-specific) features unifying persons. Universal factors also fit here, all evidencing historical or developmental exigencies. The second (subjective) is seen entailing comparatively (not entirely) quantitive, supplemental-variable, particularizing capacities diversifying persons. As created persons, humans possess such objective and subjective resources on a profoundly intensive and extensive scale. Their generically enriched substantial-spiritual faculties, with proportionately enhanced supplemental-corporeal organs, afford them nearly unlimited access to advances along the two parallel personal lines. This holds true at least, so far as a duly deferential balance between the contrasting sectors persists. That predominantly spiritual, qualitive, objective condition inherently inclines these self-transcending agents toward each other, especially emphasizing enduring, mutually expansive relationships. They thus properly display thoroughly integrating traits, personally and socially (societal), seeking ever more wholesome fulfillment through adequately consolidated, commonly controlling, personal commitments.[10]

For Berger, and the preceding similarly bodily bound analysts, however, those suprasensible distinguishing attributes have no meaning. Consequent upon their crucial biological bind, quality and quanity mainly imply variations of degree rather than kind. Subjective accordingly suggests a single individual self or acting (pseudoperson) having quite limited dynamic possibilities, chiefly numerically considered. Objective indicates the same separate individuals, multiplied and socialized, or interacting. The contrasting views therefore principally represent functional differences affecting interdependent units, as smaller and larger involvements. They merely manifest technical "positional," "historical" states, lacking substantial "dispositional," ontological import. The resultant societal combinations comprise multi-independently or individualistically inclined members, with mutual convenience taking precedence over common unifying obligations.[11]

Such a utilitarian arrangement, when normally working, effectively balances individuals (pseudopersons) exercising "institutionalizing" and "legitimating" power concertedly ("in groups"), alongside (if not against) others more or less likewise linked ("out groups"), in sharply competitive and conflictive relations.[12] Since no guiding norms and values regulating the human condition are available, beyond what these groups make themselves, the rules governing the "contest" continually change. Majority agreement concerning plausibility, under current technical, "positional" circumstances, determines legitimate institutional status. The "common good" is only the opportunity to exploit one's own "higher" bodily urges, by ways and means that entail the least cost to others' "objective" and objectionable interference.[13]

The crucial vital factor fostering correct conceptions regarding human society's reality thus coincides with the central constitutional component characterizing real personal human beings. As the former obviously flowers from the latter, through their seried supporting connections, the ensuing social systems must reflect those so committed participants' personalized living impact. We have seen how that truly telling, or critically distinguishing, human feature evidences a moderately blended, spiritual-corporeal formal or structural content. This thoroughly consolidated substantive state follows upon humanity's mediate creaturely generic position—between the lower physical-biological, and the higher angelic classes, cosmically measured. It similarly supplies the main integrating impulsions holding these profoundly, as personally, sociable agents together.[14]

We have noted, too, human nature's predominant spiritual capacity for a consciously consistent, freely posited, exercise of generalizing-specializing, ultimately universalizing (more or less transcendental) integrative tendencies. Such inherited abilities aptly systematically control accompanying corporeal, heavily materially weighted, particularizing, separating trends. The superior, intangible, intellectual-volitional faculties directly represent their possessors' relatively personalizing share in the divine, pure and perfect personal spiritual life. Humans thereby gain a proportionate, as moderate or mediate, access to reality's infinite perfecting aspects. Those total vital qualities are refracted through themselves, and the other contingent beings (angelical and physical-biological) deriving from the divine creative largess invigorating all. They simultaneously reasonably recognize the limited dynamic resources that each of them enjoys personally, and the persistent need for continuous close support mutually, if progress toward adequate self-realization would be achieved. That essential developmental potential, divinely given existentially, and objectively understandable humanly, constitutes the common good. It accordingly reflects an "open invitation" for personal fulfillment—involving a jointly and severally responsible endeavor at discovering and actualizing the divinely implanted natural capacities permeating the whole. As a real and most relevant natural dynamism, therefore, transcending while including the concrete personal constituents, this common good provides the basic bond insuring society's stability and virility.[15]

When truly discerned, such common good must be accepted, interpreted, and applied reasonably or humanly—in a manner preserving and promoting the collective members' personal integrity (individually-subjectively and communally-objectively), besides fostering the societal entity's due superiority. Thence rise critical practical problems: determining the common good's less generic and more specific implications on various vital levels; and correctly correlating it with the pertinent personal good of affected members. A fundamental obstacle here entails excessively emphasizing the latter, even when the former is apparently exaggerated. Manifesting humans' disorderly propensities, private interests—prominently particularized subjective concerns, tend to prevail over public or unified objective obligations. Secondary (individual) personal qualities thus subvert primary (communal) ones, whether done coarsely or decorously.[16]

That subversion occurs rather openly, so relatively honestly, under a social system frankly favoring individualism. It flourishes covertly, hence really hypocritically, under a social system ostensibly (often ornately) stressing the common good, but actually accentuating elitism. This partisan rule by specialists—political, cultural, scientific, artistic (group egoism), characterizes collectivism's different types. A somewhat similar situation exists in supposedly moderate societies where secularism and pluralism hold sway. Their combined, corporeally concentrated, autonomously authenticated effect encourages a subtle, sedate and discrete, cryptoindividualistic yet authoritarian professionalism. Such was seen the case as regards the ''substitious'' or substitutional scientific societal stance that we considered previously. The common error basically evident there, respectively, involves envisioning and interpreting society, and those who comprise it, chiefly corporeally, or along sensibly controlling lines, practically anyway. While affecting abstract or elemental human attitudes theoretically—either emphasizing idealistic notions of communal loyalty, or romantic conceptions of individual (pseudopersonal) independence, the concrete applications reflect adjustments to more or less pseudosophisticated individualistic ''animal'' types. Collectivists utilize the common herding approach. Individualists (overt or covert) employ the common baiting arrangement. Each way, society represents a great ''range,'' with high-grade ''stock'' adroitly competitively maneuvered, by like strenuously competitively aligned leaders.

If we would counter and correct these wileful and woeful societal aberrations, human nature's duly blended, spiritual-corporeal substantive condition must be recognized and respected. Only through this radical ''recombinative'' alteration, properly as moderately balanced, can those essentially ''middle class'' creatures regain their life-insuring, adequately organic status. Although the crux of the problem exists here, at the crucial structural or formal level, its vital import includes the prior purposeful or final, and the subsequent procedural or functional sectors also. As we observed earlier, humans' constitutive faculties, spiritual and corporeal, activate themselves on that triple-tiered dynamic scale. We saw, too, how such a fundamental overall synthesis marks both the persons and the societal strains they naturally develop. The said personal agents and collective institutions were then found to be further fully and finely equipped, consonant with vastly enhanced mental and moral abilities derived from the Christian, consummate supernatural revelation. Focussed upon the societal scene, these infinitely improved cognitive-affective facilities foster a growing awareness concerning its additional reflection of the Trinitarian impress evident in human nature, beyond the personal limits. Those more comprehensive, natural and supernatural capacities for development, collectively and personally, comprise society's common good.

The common good accordingly entails the vital potentials essentially characterizing humanity, hence critically affecting each person, and each societal agency, proportionately. It consequently is an objective reality having subjective ramifications, especially when overtly actualized. Reflecting the mainly spiritual substantive resources pertinent to its personal constituents, their intrinsic inclinations, the common good possesses what may aptly be termed a semisubstantial reality, as does the society thus demanded.[17] Correlated with our previous insights regarding Christ's Trinitarian role as Son-Word, and their societal implications, this common good specifies still more His divine creative-redemptive impact on humans. Envisioning such controlling connections adequately, not simply ecclesially, we understand better the basis of St. Paul's call for concerted communal service—whereby we form "that perfect man who is Christ come to full stature."[18]

NOTES

1. Messner, *Social Ethics*, pp. 101–104.
2. Parsons, *Social Systems*, p. 236.
3. Parsons, *System of Modern Societies*, pp. 6–11.
4. Parsons, *Social Systems*, p. 312.
5. MacIver, *Society*, p. 511.
6. Ibid., pp. 49–50.
7. Sorokin, *Society, Culture and Personality*, pp. 342–343.
8. Ibid., p. 63.
9. Berger, *The Social Construction of Reality*, p. 129.
10. Messner, *Social Ethics*, pp. 97–100. Cf. J. Maritain, *The Person and the Common Good*, Chapter III (New York: Scribner, 1947).
11. Berger, *Social Construction of Reality*, Part II.
12. Ibid., pp. 108–110, 182–183.
13. Ibid., pp. 52, 78.
14. Cf. Maritain, *The Person and the Common Good*, pp. 28–34.
15. Ibid., pp. 37–45. Cf. Messner, *Social Ethics*, pp. 104–107.
16. Maritain, *The Person and the Common Good*, pp. 49–66.
17. Messner, *Social Ethics*, pp. 117–150.
18. Eph. 4:11–13.

Part V

Chapter Eleven

SOCIETY'S ADDITIONAL SPIRITUAL IMPLICATIONS

As explained earlier, the Church affords the societal community (local, regional, national, and international) the spiritual-moral standards, supernatural and natural, safe-guiding and guarding human beings' development. That may be done either patently (direct avowal) or latently (indirect approval). These crucial normative contributions principally insure the recipients' essential integrity amid myriad variable existential conditions. They do so by consistently promoting a proper personal balance in the affected agents' diverse dynamic relationships, individual and collective. We have seen how this means maintaining an apt spiritual (generic-specific, objective-qualitive) control over corporeal (particular-subjective-quantitive) counterparts. It likewise was seen to require one's extending such constitutional symmetry throughout the triple-seried dynamism (ends, means, methods) that basically activates the thus consolidated creature. Those elementary vital obligations apply initially at the individual, semi-personal level. As similarly noted before, they subsequently impinge upon the societal plane, exerting a still more significant or much enhanced personalizing impact there. Three distinct (not separate) mutually supporting collective sectors accordingly are projected appropriately and fundamentally—religious-political, cultural-familial, economic fine arts—mundane arts. Each so vertically aligned dynamic division is additionally vitally distinguished (not separated) horizontally, as it were, or more interiorly and more exteriorly concentrated respectively. The latter differences follow from comparative connections with human nature's spiritual and corporeal content.

Although the said constitutional components and developmental framework comprise humanity's essential core, manifesting the divine Trinitarian creative impress, their consciously meaningful correlation largely has been lost, if ever truly understood. Opting for a "do it yourself" analytic-synthetic interpretive approach, humans historically have alternated between primitive objective superstitious, and innovative subjective "substitious" naturalistic extremes. Only since Christ's authentic (directly divinely given) supernatural revelationn occurred, did the way out of this debilitating darkness become available. He provided the crucial mediating truth (fulfilling that begun in Judaism), whereby whoever believes Him can overcome the crippling ideological and idolatrous worldly-wise contrivances stressing self-satisfaction. He continues such mainly moral-spiritual liberation chiefly through His authoritively established societal agency, the Catholic Church. It dutifully and decisively expands while extending Christ's saving thoroughly moderating message amid peoples' varied vital strivings worldwide.

We also observed previously how the Church's critically saving influence on society ultimately exhibits the same systematic course that Christ evidenced—"the way, the truth, and the life." We likewise saw how the summary statement symbolizes both His mediating personal role in the Trinity, and His especially close divinely incarnate relationship with human beings, the mediate or middle creaturely class. Implicitly too, it reflects His peculiar mediate creative impact, as the divine Son-Word, upon the latter. This wholesome dynamic order depicts Christ's distinctive Trinitarian vitalizing contribution, therefore; the second

Person who formulates the truth that projects the life flowing from the first Person, and promotes the way fostered by the third Person. Though the profoundly perfecting process for humanity was inaugurated along individual-personal lines, out of natural necessity, it carries corresponding societal-communal import. Founding and commissioning the Church stressed such essential connection. So did the additional admonition, "the man who has faith in me will do the works I do, and greater far than these."[1]

As affecting human personal relations individually considered, the crucial core in the truth Christ conveyed became evident when He said, "The spirit gives life, the flesh is useless." That fundamental vital formula, and the generally disregarded discipline it demands, constitutes His messianic message's central theme—"Reform your lives." Only thus can one achieve the humanly fulfilling condition that characterizes a person. Actually adapting to the spiritually controlling moral standards summarily expressed through the "beatitudes" alone insures its accomplishment. Those accordingly reformed then possess the potently balanced faculties or means, facilitating like properly blended functional alternatives (giving over getting) or methods, thereby fostering the ultimate personalized goal (eternal life). Consonant with human beings mediate or "middle class" creaturely status, between the angelic and physico-biologic generic types, the salvific process' middle term—truth-means, holds main significance (meaning). Mediation or moderation—adequately as spiritually discriminating (reasoning, not corporeally compromised rationalizing) decision—determines humanity's wholesome success.

This critical human vital order has been seen deriving from, hence especially reflecting, the divine Son-Word's somewhat extra-close creative import for such "second class" creatures. It consequently remotely represents His mediating relationship to the divine Father and Holy Spirit. We further noted earlier how the divine vitalizing impact upon human nature cannot be realized thoroughly at the individualized personal level. The former's fuller enrichening effusions entail increasingly concentrated consolidating linkings—sexual, racial, and societal. These more comprehensive personalizing qualities refract or extend the basic human dynamic outlined above. They therefore have the same fundamental suitability for supernatural enhancement by Christ's redemptive contributions.

In the societal community, or the principal collective species aptly integrated, humanity's constitutionally balanced share of reality's developmental dynamism (ends, means, methods) is manifested through the religious-political, cultural-familial, economic fine arts-mundane arts synthesis. As the mediate, overall structural, means sector, the cultural-familial combinations exercise the main unifying or organizing influence. They do so, however, under the religious-political sector's due, general orienting, purposeful directions. Those middle stratum societal units thus dimly depict, more exactly than on the personal plane, Christ's most typical personal vital responses (as Son-Word) to the Father's divine guiding designs. The cultural-familial combines exert a similar stimulating effect upon the succeeding, comparatively operating, typically procedural (methods) societal sector—economic fine arts-mundane arts. These very practical agencies likewise properly follow the religious-political authoritys' relatively theoretical directional indications. This last-stage dual dynamic reaction more nearly reflects the Holy Spirit's appropriate active, divine alignment with the Son-Word and the Father respectively.

Together, then, such inherently complementary, mutually invigorating, jointly systematized connections foster the societal community's essential common good. Correctly conceived and interpreted (through a reasonable correlation of natural experience and supernatural revelation), and correspondingly implemented responsibly, they proportionately increase the divine Trinity's enlivening import for human relationships. The Divinity's infinite resourcefulness is shown here, as at the other vital levels (racial, sexual, personal), by the quantitatively limitless variety flourishing amid those qualitatively controlling boundaries. Although the human person's predominantly spiritual substance displays evolutionary tendencies also, due to the total being's contingency, it evidences still more an innate participation in the divine unifying immensity. If the particularizing corporeal organs change entirely, eventually disintegrating, the spirit's generalizing-specializing, ultimately universalizing faculties maintain an abiding albeit progressively actualized consistency. When adequately disciplined—integrally, objectively, communally inclined components decisively ordering separately, subjectively, individually centered counterparts—we have the wholesomely developed mediate personal creature. That redemptive completion requires consummating radical reformation through corporeal death and subsequent spiritualized resurrection. Humans' essential-existential thrust toward perfection can be frustrated, by consciously and freely rejecting the responsibility that their spiritual impress seriously imposes.

We should consider, summarily anyway, some additional relevant societal ramifications (natural and supernatural) of the foregoing fundamental constitutional dynamism vitalizing human nature. This principally spiritual, but supplementally corporeal, initial impelling force provides the protective and promotive drives fostering the concrete personal agents' development. Such original "action system" (Parsons's primal theme), what aptly may be termed the created "trialectic" (ends, means, methods), represents the divine Trinity's personal impact upon humanity. When correctly recognized and respected, consonant with these mediate level creatures' reasonable freedom, it insures an endlessly enduring and ennobling life. We have seen how the said crucial vital syndrome is exemplified societally by the religious-political, cultural-familial, and economic fine arts–mundane arts sectors. That merely reflects the view from the top, one might properly say. The same supernatural-natural systematizing force weaves its enlivening effects still more integrally and intricately inside each societal species.

NOTE

1. John 14:12.

Chapter Twelve

GENERAL RAMIFICATIONS

RELIGIOUS AND POLITICAL RAMIFICATIONS

Religious and political societies, as chiefly spiritual and corporeal purposeful or orienting agencies respectively, for the total societal community, have their own distinct (not separate) goals. The former mainly emphasizes the overall membership's eternal welfare, while the latter works similarly on the temporal plane. They necessarily interrelate, because of the members' spiritually-corporeally combined constitution. The two parallel collective types manifest correspondingly balanced priorities among essentially divisible ends—ultimate, mediate, proximate. Each likewise exhibits a comparably correlated structural order, where complementary consolidating positions (tentatively termed ''planners,'' ''programmers,'' ''promoters'') are discernible. The standard ''trialectical'' connection accordingly persists here, and in a thoroughly organic manner.

Thus, the Church has bishops, who approximate ''planners'' determining ultimate spiritual ends, under subsequently stated conditions. Priests, religious, and specially qualified laity exercise mediate level spiritual authority as ''programmers.'' The other lay members perform various proximate spiritual services as ''promoters.'' Further indicating the ''trialectic's'' intricate integrative import, the prior ''planners' '' initiating influence naturally includes a certain supervisory control over the two succeeding constituencies. ''Programmers'' have proportionate authoritative responsibilities toward ''promoters.'' This penetrating consistency does not derogate from the several classes equally beneficial roles. Rather is it a case of priority amid parity, since neither organizational part can do without the counterparts; anymore than the preceding basic purposeful divisions (ultimate, mediate, proximate) may be collapsed. We see again, then, the divine Trinitarian relations remotely imaged in the somewhat complex, as partly composite because contingent, human creaturely category.

The State also has primary, purposeful authorities who constitute ultimate corporeal ''planners'' or legislators; mediate stage, structural officials who comprise its corporeal ''programmers'' or judges; and proximate agents, executives, who work closer to ordinary citizens as corporeal ''promoters.'' These ''trialectic'' relationships are actively integrated along temporal ordering lines, paralleling the eternal ecclesial kind already mentioned. Priorities between equals properly prevail here too. Such qualitative distinctions obviously have accompanying quantitative aspects, on a correspondingly concerted as well as contrasting scale, both for Church and State. They principally reflect larger or smaller concrete societal dimensions, like local, regional, and national. Area and authoritative differences characterizing the Church normally display less frequency than those marking the State. The former's comparatively reduced number of regulatory agents and agencies indicates the human spirit's fundamentally stronger synthesizing capacities, in contrast to the body's.

Another crucial subtle distinction regarding the religious and political societal sectors' essential constituencies should be stressed. As we observed earlier, the overall positional priority possessed by these goal-determining institutions does not afford them main importance. Consonant with human nature's mediate creaturely status—intervening anent the angelic and physical-biological created genera, its mediate formational societal units (cultural-familial) fill the critical consolidating role (what Parsons termed "pattern-maintenance"). Angels chiefly concentrate upon ends or goals, while physical-biological types proportionately emphasize methods or functions. This primordial vital fact was seen confirmed, implicitly at least, through Christ's revelation concerning His mediative meaning for humanity. He mainly urged reforming efforts, as the central move towards renewing the latter's fallen natural condition. That basically entailed showing them the key truth (spirit's dominion over body), which opens the way leading to eternal life. The middle-level dynamic factor—form, structure or means (adequately considered), therefore carries extra saving significance on the human plane, personally and societally.

Like the mediate cultural-familial species exerting the telling structural developmental influence in the societal community (under religious-political species' proper purposeful guidance), so do the mediate constituencies of each such species rightfully exercise an analogous invigorating impact. Ecclesially viewed, then, the priests-religious-lay leaders' moral-spiritual mediating position (as teachers linking theory with practice) closes the vital circuit between the bishops' principles and the laitys' actions. A similar important connecting responsibility is held by the official political "programmer" or middle class. Judicial and quasi-judicial authorities—judges, civil-legal scholars, lawyers, as especially competent interpreters, make the legislature's principles practically meaningful for executives and the general citizenry.

The "trialectic" dynamism obviously impregnates these societal species' procedural processes. Lawmaking, interpreting, and applying undergird their members' rationally (reasonably) ordered relationships. Those public operations extend the fundamental religious and political values-norms that wholesomely inspire the membership. The said central conceptions derive from the accumulated collective traditions respectfully received, reactivated and readjusted consistently in each succeeding generation.

For the Church, this means the supernaturally revealed truths (Scriptural) made available through its divine Founder, and authentically announced since then (dogmas). In the State, such "supreme law of the land" is represented by controlling constitutional norms. Again we find notable differences characterizing the two guiding societal agencies. The religious institution's more durable, universal, mainly spiritual-moral (supplementally canonical) directives display a sharp contrast to the political unit's civil-legal, largely changeable, comparatively regional standards (indirectly or basically moral). They reflect the former's qualitive, spiritual superiority over the latter's prominently quantitative, corporeal services. They also reflect the former's official link to God explicitly, rather than implicitly, as the other societies.

Concerning channels of reciprocal interaction, the natural order would follow a "like-to-like" relationship. Bishops, as ecclesial "planners," ordinarily communicate with their civil counterparts—legislators. Priests-religious-lay leaders, or ecclesial "programmers," customarily contact political opposites —judges, legal scholars, lawyers. The Church's laity correspondingly concentrate upon the State's executives. However, considering the essential equality marking the several constituencies in each parallel societal species (religious-political), conditions can allow, even require, alternate approaches avoiding proper priorities.

CULTURAL AND FAMILIAL RAMIFICATIONS

Cultural and familial groupings, being relatively natural, spiritual and corporeal structural or organizing components of the total societal community respectively, exert proportionately distinct (not separate) developmental influences. The first type especially emphasizes the collective membership's comprehensive natural spiritual formation (intellectual-volitional disciplines on an overall philosophic-scientific-artistic scale), or thorough universal-generic-specific education. The second chiefly stresses a more particularized (imaginative-sensitive-vegetative) natural corporeal educational development. A mutual overlapping obviously occurs essentially, as was seen the case with the religious and political societies. Cultural formative contributions, although principally very objective and substantive, necessarily impinge upon subjective, supplementive features. Similarly, familial formational services, while primarily individually inclined, simultaneously involve overriding common human linkages. They thus closely intertwine, due to their members' spiritual-corporeal, moderately or mediately blended content. Both parallel societal agencies accordingly exhibit complementally differentiated goals, of an ultimate, mediate, and proximate kind. As mainly spiritual, cultural benefits are more eternally enduring than the pronouncedly temporal or corporeal familial sort. Both also manifest like-structured constituents peculiarly adept at advancing those ends. Fundamentally filling the same consolidating roles as religious-political counterparts, we may conveniently give them identical titles—"planners," "programmers," "promoters." The crucial "trialectic" dynamism consequently is further refracted here.

Before additionally examining these key cultural characteristics, it seems advisable that we clarify better such societal species' general collective import, as presently envisioned. Consistent with this study's concentration on mediation, or a middle-level vital approach, we view the said human reality along much the same analytical lines. Our conception of culture must be distinguished from a most general type, wherein humanity's total productive patterns are directly included. It likewise differs from an opposing, most specific usage: when the term entails a very concrete situation, exemplified by a biological experimental "culture." A mediate position between those extremes is assumed instead. More or less encompassing humans' universal vital interests indirectly, as correlated in a historical context, and a generic-specific, philosophic-scientific-artistic interpretive synthesis, that knowledgeable heritage comprises society's main or mediate formational resource. Such richly enlightening reservoir has been accumulated through energetic investigation, systematized to produce the various informative disciplines. Adequately considered, supernaturally as well as naturally, the latter aptly reflect properly proportioned spiritual-moral integrating influences of the Church (theological). Possessing predominantly spiritual (intellectual-volitional) significance, these cultural components, and their carrying agencies, have an intrinsic connection with the Church. Contrarily, the State's corporeally concentrated contributions rightly have only extrinsic effects, ordinarily.

Because the societal community's cultural species inherently adopt a fuller comprehensive attitude toward the realities they study, and also the persons they serve, than do either the religious or political types, this requires more numerous principal outlets on the formers' part. The fact holds especially as regards the Church, somewhat less so concerning the State. Those greater complexities generate extra difficulties in discerning the basic "trialectic" imprint among the membership. Clearly, many characteristic combinations are involved here, having fundamentally related but supplementally disparate roles. They vary from small-scale comparatively specialized research, scholarly training centers, to the large, extended educational institutions, like colleges and universities. Fairly representative, generally relevant constituencies may be distinguished along the aforenoted elemental dynamic lines. Faculty councils serve as "planners," departmental teaching staff exemplify "programmers," and executive staff, together with the receiving participants or students, provide "promoters." "Trustees' " dominant supervisory status demonstrates an extrinsic impact of the State's civil-legal authority.

Remotely reflecting the divine Trinity's infinite integral dynamism, closer consolidating connections between the basic societal classes exist at this cultural level also. Essential equality naturally marks all three, since each shares the others' human prerogatives. They evidence the usual proportionate complementary priorities too. Though ultimate internal control is exercised by the "planners," "programmers" and "promoters" possess a due autonomy and responsibility. Human nature's critical mediating onus again places special stress upon "programmers," as noted previously when examining the religious and political units. Their typical structuring contributions here hold even greater significance than the corresponding kind in the preceding purposeful societal sector. Because cultural agencies actually supply the total community's main organic services ("pattern-maintenance")—concomitantly with the familial, such associations' "programmers" have the most overall integrating impact. Those chiefly spiritual (intellectual-volitional) formational benefits, presumably enriched supernaturally through apt ecclesial guidance, mainly make societal life meaningful. Producing adequately organized instructional programs (general or special), which facilitate a fuller comprehensive understanding of reality, or thorough teaching (visually or vocally), comprise the central cultural role. "Planners' " prior guiding, and "promoters' " subsequent supporting, aid accordingly complement the middle, mediating constituency.

Focussing now on the familial side of the societal community's mediate dynamic sector, we likewise discern the Trinitarian "trialectic" impress there. Whether viewing that society more traditionally, as jointly arranged, or more modernistically, as independently founded, the "planners," "programmers," and "promoters" obviously persist. Wives ordinarily perform the first duty, husbands the second, and younger or older offspring the third. Women normally are better equipped psychologically for planning or guiding activity. Men similarly display inherent inclinations toward mediating or organizing involvements. Children, juvenile and later ages at least, regularly exhibit extra agility in executing or completing tasks. As with the foregoing collective species, here too the essential constitutencies manifest a certain mutual flexibility. While the respective characteristic traits prevail generally, each somewhat supplementally shares the others' fundamentally human capacities. Although a duly proportionate authoritative precedence properly exists between the family's members, a reciprocal autonomy and responsibility also applies. Matching their societal counterparts, priority amid parity is the rule.

Again we observe the mediate "programmers' " (husband's) crucial consolidating contributions. Husbands or fathers provide the vital structural influence, linking the wives' or mothers' purposeful articulations, and the progeny's procedural assistance. Furthermore, paralleling their cultural opposites, these familial "programmers" enjoy an extension of the latters' additional mediative import, attendant upon the middle sectors' main overall developmental service to the total societal community. Being so materially embellished, however, because reflecting that community's corporeal content prominently, and its comprehensive connecting or mediating aspect besides, those "trialectic" domestic relationships are not readily recognizable. The same large-scale tangible temporal features unite the familial society comparatively close with the political one, representing an intrinsic natural tie. It resembles the cultural complement's inherent inclination toward the religious agency. Nonetheless, the Church's supernatural spiritual-moral impact ultimately correctly governs families, as it similarly regulates political and cultural combinations.

The familial training role, which intensifies its corporeal procreating and nurturing one, especially emphasizes the members' particular personal condition. This necessarily includes inculcating objective principles, but as more exactly befitting their recipients' individual subjective abilities. Such radically diverse needs stem from the bodily organism's vastly varied material capacities, vitally synthesized through accompanying superior spiritual faculties. The resultant sharply blended, qualitatively and quantitatively, personal agents require intimately particularized corporeal services for adequate development. Families exist largely to supply these structurally individualized aids. They thus greatly outnumber, in total outer extent, the fuller spiritualized, hence proportionately stronger unified, parallel cultural societies. On that contrasting count, then, the differences between those jointly mediating societal species roughly approximate the relative quantitative content distinguishing the prior purposeful collective counterparts (religious-political). A corresponding qualitative distinction simultaneously applies there, and so should be given proper recognition. Since the cultural associations mainly constitute spiritual formational centers, naturally considered, they rightly exercise a certain disciplinary suzerainty over the family's characteristically corporeal contributions (like Church and State).

ECONOMIC FINE ARTS' AND MUNDANE ARTS' RAMIFICATIONS

The Trinitarian "trialectic" completes its dynamic socializing impulsions by spawning and supporting human nature's typical procedural societal sector. As noted earlier, economic groupings chiefly provide services that comparatively comprise collective methods facilitating the efforts of cultural-familial (collective means) and religious-political (collective ends) units at promoting the common good. These benefits are basically distinguishable along the same spiritual-corporeal vital lines marking the societal community as a whole. Such integrally blended generic condition is manifested on this collective functional plane through two parallel economic, or very specifically productive, typical combinations. We have labeled them, in reasonably representative terms, fine arts and mundane arts. The first principally entails spiritually connected offerings; the second primarily encompasses corporeally concentrated kinds. Evidencing the mutual reciprocity linking the other comparable societal pairs, those distinct (not separate) essential agencies interact closely. However, because especially reflecting respectively contrary constitutional elements (spiritual-corporeal), they display still stronger ties with their lineal complements. The fine arts accordingly respond more appropriately to cultural and religious influences while the mundane arts react similarly toward familial and political tendencies. Nonetheless, the overall vertical and horizontal, organically unifying bonds of the common good impose proportionate obligations—spiritual-moral and civil-legal, upon both species.

The infrastructural relationships between central constituencies within each procedural societal component exhibit some important peculiarities. Since the Trinitarian "trialectic" persists here, we find the usual crucial relational roles—"planners," "programmers," and "promoters." Activities in this functional area naturally are very specialized. A greater personal autonomy than the degree allowed by the preceding sectors consequently characterizes these involvements. Such clearly is the case among the exponents of the fine arts anyway, although not quite so conspicuously amid mundane artistic engagements. Exceptional independent productive skills spark the formers' accomplishments, initially or directly at least. The thus talented artists then actually fill all three fundamental dynamic demands—planning, programming, and promoting. They do this on what amounts to a quasi-collective scale (servicing public interests and needs), as distinct from merely articulating the said dynamism privately. Aptly assuming and performing that concerted societal task provides the true basis for the artists' fame.

Obviously, the resultant compositions' completion requires more than their originators' efforts. Without additional mediating assistance, the personally produced works ordinarily cannot have an adequate public effect. Whether entailing attendant expertise approximating the composers, or a rather supplementary technical sort, this representative support carries critical value. It really contributes much toward "making" or "breaking" the principal product. Others consequently share the "trialectic" burden, which the prime producer pioneered. While the latter normally retain the main responsibilities as "planners" and "programmers," subsequent collaborators supply telling aid of comparatively equal significance, as "promoters." Only through such socializing processes will the independent initiator possibly achieve societal success. Priority amid parity largely remains the rule here, even if seemingly stretched somewhat.

Regarding priorities, again we find the mediating or programming division holding crucial import. That consolidating constituency continues to evidence the chief meaningful impact upon humans, as creation's middle class. It likewise continues working these especially relevant benefits amid the prior planning and posterior promoting influences. The entire fine arts' ensemble also rightly respects the Church's pertinent spiritual-moral, and the State's proper civil-legal overall societal guidance. Being decisively spiritually formed, fine arts are intrinsically inclined toward the cultural and religious species. They are relatively extrinsically affected by accompanying corporeal counterparts—mundane arts, familial, political. Reflecting society's procedural dynamism, and its essentially detailed, prominently quantitative features, the fine arts naturally generate more numerous outlets than either of their spiritual complements —cultural-religious. Such diversified dispensings predominate most noticeably in the products profusely supplied.

The mundane arts comprise the societal community's economic or procedural species on the corporeal side. Those detailed productive contributions principally aim at satisfying people's bodily needs, directly or indirectly. They thus parallel the fine arts' pronouncedly spiritual services. They similarly yet surpassingly manifest the latters' quantitatively heavy marks, because so strongly corporeal. That is the case, not only concerning diverse productions, but includes the human producers involved. The two numerically expansive tendencies reciprocally reinforce each other. As already mentioned, opportunities for autonomous, innovative activity abound there, rather closely resembling the fine arts. However, these independent engagements usually have less qualitative value, due to reduced spiritual content. An additional very significant difference follows from this fuller bodily blend. Since human endeavors then are potently charged corporeally, hence entail a high degree of largely mechanical or merely repetitious commitment, they can be combined conveniently and efficiently in extremely centralized enterprises. On the same account, such regularized roles often will be replaced altogether by automatic machines. The mammoth industrial complexes that result help explain how relatively few (measured against the familial) economic agencies catering to the mundane arts supply so many products.

As with the fine arts, the intimate relationship between a project's originator and its implementing collaborators prevails here, approximately anyway. Approximation seems like an apt description because important differences exist. The original mundane artistic projections ordinarily do not possess the representational thoroughness that normally characterize fine artistry. They generally match the latter's import, though, as initial outline and near-complete work respectively. The former's fuller features thus become clearly realized only after subsequent experimentation. This ''learning while doing'' approach actually typifies the procedural societal sector on the whole. Its emphatically pragmatic attitude is accentuated all the more in the mundane area through an axiomatic corporeal concentration. Although those very transient, technically ambivalent factors facilitate extensive quantitative combinations, complementary qualitative or spiritual connections rightly receive controlling stress. Such a crucial vital balance holds especially for the principal participants—overseeing originators (employers) and underserving operators (employees).

The Trinitarian ''trialectic'' syndrome, ''planners,'' ''programmers,'' and ''promoters,'' persists amid these economic mundane arts also. Properly paralleling the fine arts' organic articulating arrangements, projects' originators, or their authorized agents, enjoy a certain privileged planning status. However, since the relevant reality encompassed by the initiating contributions has a high corporeal content, and correspondingly low enduring portent, the authoritative innovators' priority does not carry quite the same significance as the spiritually profound fine artists. Proportionately increased contingencies limit more stringently the starting impulsions' imposing import. Subsequent operational experience and experiment, on greater and lesser collaborative scales, afford them continuing progressive assistance. While the ''founders'' and their enteprising successors still exercise a duly respected planning primacy, they prudently expect improving proposals from earnest employees. This entails closer integral relationships between ''planners'' and the other essential constituencies (''programmers,'' ''promoters''). Priority amid parity patently applies here. The resultant relational informality reflects the mundane arts' inherently intimate, natural (corporeal) alignment with the familial and political societal species. It thus balances the somewhat more formal, similar natural (spiritual) ties of the fine arts to cultural and religious counterparts. Nonetheless, besides accepting the State's civil-legal properly proportioned temporal tutelage, the mundane arts additionally recognize the Church's similar spiritual-moral eternal suzerainty.

Despite the very pertinent prominence accorded the mundane arts' basically contrasting contributors—originators and operators, the mediating organizers or ''programmers'' perform the main role. As in the preceding societal combinations, then, adequate development depends upon how well that critical requirement is fulfilled. The problem's complications are comparatively reduced among the fine arts, because a stronger spiritual outlook and output fosters the needed negotiating attitude there. Mutual benefits accompanying such accommodating arrangements can be seen better, aided, partly at least, by significantly subdued quantitative elements. Those favorable features obviously decline when entering the mundane arts' realm. They still remain, though, if proportionately diluted, available and exploitable through reasonable or responsible conduct.

The crux of the problem concerning programming control in the mundane arts hinges around the fact that the originating artists' initiating contributions do not possess thoroughly decisive content. As noted above, these inaugural contrivances contain merely the "seeds," one might say, of the intended enterprise. This is decidedly different from the fine arts' central systematizing component. The latter determines the succeeding joint endeavors quite distinctly, leaving largely supplementary rather than complementary actualizing opportunities for the subsequent collaborators. What overtly ensues can be called correctly the originators' "work." It receives necessary publicizing aid through truly sympathetic supporting artistic attention. Contrarily, mundane productive initiators provide only a framework, so to speak, which demands further filling before becoming an identifiable entity. The resulting composite accordingly exhibits more or less equal vital sources. Both contributing participants (originators-operators) consequently deserve correspondingly relevant, reciprocally authoritative dynamic roles.

Some may say that the mundane artistic involvement represents a continuous kind, while the fine arts' engagements are relatively momentary. The observation's apparent accuracy reflects the radical distinction between corporeal and spiritual vitality. The latter's products, being more substantial and durable, do not require the same constant reproduction and replacement characterizing the former's transient type. However, the fine arts' projects also display, secondarily or marginally, some of the tangible temporal factors properly intrinsic to their mundane opposites, and vice versa. As explained earlier, such overlapping follows from the intimate, intricate unity interlacing human nature's spiritual-corporeal elements.

Programming in the mundane arts should be pursued along closely combined, comparatively equivalent participating lines therefore. Under this mutually respectful arrangement, originators and operators are realistically consolidated as the crucial organic constituency (''programmers''). That dynamic synthesis then insures a proportionate balance at the planning and promoting levels. As likewise observed previously, the founding authors, or agents thereof, still rightly enjoy a certain precedence on all three planes, consistent with the essential ''trialectic'' vital order entailing priority amid parity. Needless to say, where distinct financial investors become involved, they should have a due representation, in promotional affairs anyway. Naturally, the said synthesized programming condition does not necessarily include all employers and employees immediately. Responsibly selected and directed representatives ordinarily perform the proximately pertinent, mediately common tasks.

The foregoing chiefly qualitative integrating effects of the Trinitarian ''trialectic's'' supernatural vitalizing impact upon the societal community carries corresponding quantitative benefits, concretely considered. Human development is not merely thus promoted more thoroughly through diverse, temporally and spatially disparate, communal establishments (local, regional, national). Those various limited searches and services for the true common good intrinsically tend toward reciprocally expanding and intensifying living links. Human beings' universalistic vital urge, infinitely enhanced by the consciously impregnating and invigorating divine dynamism (ends, means, methods), seeks ever wider, as well as wiser, mutually completing and jointly contributing (to the full common good) combinations. This spiritually controlled unifying trend affects both personal and societal attitudes, within a corporeal context. The Church's universalizing example, theoretical and practical, provides patent and potent assistance here. Though the effort may seem utopian from a worldly viewpoint, it has actual vital value for all who ''make it.'' They then share the ''more abundant'' eternal life that Christ came to give; here and now, perfectingly, but hereafter perfectly.

Chapter Thirteen

ADDITIONAL SPIRITUAL IMPLICATIONS OF CHRISTIAN REVELATION

Our reflections on Christ's salvific or supernaturally revitalizing role, as it influences the societal community, largely have emphasized cognitive or theoretical implications. The truth-full way insuring permanent life that He originally offered, and continuously offers vicariously through His Church, has been analyzed primarily along conceptual lines, as principles. Such stress was necessary, obviously, in the course of facilitating understanding, humans' initial, guiding vital approach. Unless so essentially enlightened priorly, these profoundly rational agents cannot otherwise participate properly. We noted at the study's start, however, and subsequently reaffirmed periodically, another personal component's equal importance. It practically complements, under the basically common creaturely dynamic—priority amid parity, the innately preceding, cognizing or theorizing one. Adopting Parsons's very appropriate classification here, we term cognition's conscious counterpart affection. Interpreted more penetratingly, philosophically, and theologically, and reciprocally related to understanding, this empowering responsive state is labeled loving.

Those contrasting yet radically completing conditions are represented by similarly significant alternate articulations, like thought and expression, light and power. The intimately and intricately interacting processes thus indicated reflect mutually reinforcing vital impulsions issuing from organs and faculties comprising human nature's upper and under organic levels. Both fundamental developmental exigencies constantly, if not always consistently, generate the activities characterizing each person. As we observed earlier, they essentially entail the interior, sub-stantial-spiritual, intellectual-volitional faculties' dynamic im-press, supplemented with the exterior, corporeal, imaginative-sensitive-vegetative capacities' parallel impact. Maintaining the formers' due constitutional superiority over the latter simulta-neously assures a person's relevant upper resources' apt active priority toward the lower set. That systematic structural balance has been stressed steadily during the foregoing investigations. It supplies the crucial (formal, mediating) alignment that mainly determines human advancement.

The Christian revelation's societal significance, as thought, light, or principle, albeit implicitly including expression, power, practice, received explicit attention in the preceding explanations. Such a theoretical approach chiefly involved correlating this doc-trine's conceptual content and the pertinent natural human dis-ciplines expounding their subjects' essential-existential condition. We then obtained a sure-guiding outline for truly progressive living on a collective or personally integrated scale. Realistic efforts at promoting personal enhancement soon show, though, how guidance alone never is enough to achieve adequate results. Understanding can be far removed from loving because of inept implementing. As humans' mental or cognitive ability depends heavily upon derived assistance for its vitality, so does the emo-tional or affective counterpart require proportionate invigorating support. Given those complementary components' fundamental unitary cohesiveness, benefits gained by one automatically infiltrate the other, elementally anyway. Nonetheless, their decidedly distinct (not separate) dynamisms demand correspondingly concentrated nurturing respectively. The problem becomes complicated tremendously through a seriously disordered relationship introduced between contrasting spiritual and corporeal faculties. These rather radically competing basic constituents—vertical (upper and under) horizontal (interior and exterior), consequently need peculiarly potent cultivation persistently, to maintain a proper mutual harmony. Since no being fails from rising too high, despite misleading superficial appearance, a frustrating vital impediment inevitably entails descending too low, or falling. The crucial human defection therefore exalts affection at the expense of cognition, accordingly preferring the former's closer corporeal connections over the latter's stronger spiritual ties.

For such very real and relevant reasons, then, Christ affords His followers distinct (not separate) instrumental symbolic means that unite them with Him intimately and personally. One type works its integrating effects on the mental or cognitive plane, as implicit ecclesial sacrament in light. The other kind serve similarly on the emotional or affective level, as explicit ecclesial sacraments in power. Joined in Christ through those essentially and existentially appropriate living links, spiritual more than corporeal, Christians experience a truly wholesome supernatural communion. They thus proportionately enjoy an eminently ennobling share of the abundant life He offers. Starting from that foundational relationship, continually renewed, they subsequently move toward its thorough realization, by consistently exploiting its additional witnessing opportunities and obligations among all who are available. This requires regular careful reflection regarding His enlightening principles intended impact upon human efforts at development under His Church's authoritative interpretive guidance. The said sharing responsibilities likewise include earnest and energetic endeavors to apply the resultant improved conceptions along individual and communal, private and public, or properly personal lines. While letting their "light shine so that others may see (the) good works and thus give glory to God" (Matt. 5:16), Christians extend their Leader's role as "salt of the earth" and "light of the world" (Matt. 5:13–14).

Especially significant examples in these combined Christocentric connections stem from the two more typical, or regularly mediating, ecclesial sacraments—Penance-Renconciliation and Eucharist-"Reconstitution." They foster the most intimate personal union with Christ, affectively considered. The supernatural enlivening power transmitted by the first patently was shown through the miraculous cures that Christ worked as symbolizing His forgiving role. It is experienced less radically, but no less reassuringly, whenever persons utilize the sacramental penitential process aptly (faithfully, hopefully, piously). "Whoever asks receives, whoever seeks finds, whoever knocks has it opened."[1] Affective enrichment accrues gradually here, initially dependent upon the recipients' persistent conscious engagement. This involves sincere admission, contrition, compensation, and correction concerning faults. Such overt acts, covertly imploring hence correspondingly incurring the ever present divine assistance, then profoundly strengthen the healed persons' respect for the enlightening word. The latter represent the life-insuring principles that overlay and securely guide both immediate and ensuing mediating endeavors.[2]

A similar, yet still stronger supernatural supporting power (under-level vitality) derives from the Eucharistic sacrament —Christ's glorified body and blood. Its spiritual meaning was signified by His miraculous feeding of the multitudes. Those astounding bodily benefitting services, rather resembling a communal self-disposal, remotely indicate what believers gain through a eucharistic union with Christ. As the enheartening blessings came to the Jews who had first accepted lengthy lessons (several days) on the new supernatural principles, thus rewarding and encouraging their mental commitment, the Eucharist's beneficiaries are likewise proportionately enriched emotionally or volitionally. This stimulates yet greater efforts at actively implementing the intellectually inspiring, life-giving, and guiding light. The whole person consequently becomes increasingly inclined toward a thoroughly supernatural commitment. Ecclesial sacraments accordingly provide under-level or virile vital power, complementing upper-level or mental vital light (Scriptural Gospels), so profoundly promoting full-scale personal living.[3]

Wholesome Christian living is much more than these and similar chiefly receptive divine relationships however. As we recalled when starting our study, such a comparatively easygoing attitude—emphasizing getting over giving—contributed enormously to the radical rending of Christ's Church. Whether excessively advocating a sanctifying faith in vicarious reparation (ecclesial techniques), or vicarious reformation (individual techniques), the same superficial sacramental prayerful (self-serving) approach prevailed. Both constitute convenient contrivances for gaining salvation surreptitiously—relying simply upon rigorous requests, while omitting, slyly, onerous obligations. Both contradict Christ's crystal-clear warning: "None of those who cry out 'Lord, Lord' will enter the kingdom of God, but only the one who does the will of my Father in heaven."[4] Temptations along those pleasantly beguiling but perniciously belittling lines have plagued the Church continally during every era. Although Christ constantly stressed the crucial need of serving others ("My Father works and I work"), emulating His own example even unto laying down one's life, many people (high and low) obstinately and obtusely prefer prayer—"letting God do it."

Christ certainly prayed, concomitantly insisting that His disciples do the same. He showed how this intimate communing with God is necessary to maintain vital integrity. He also showed how such vital integrity, in our earthly circumstances, mainly required "carrying the cross"—daily sacrifical service, which human redemption entailed. Prayer supported, and compensated, as real spiritual nourishment, the loving liberating labors. The latter attained critical consummation, not substitution, by His ultimate sacrificial service—passion and death. Their heavenly consummation became evident from the resurrection. Passion and death thus completed the preceding public ministry, putting the seal of thorough sincerity (''obedient unto death'') upon all He previously said and did. ''The good shepherd lays down his life for the sheep.''[5]

A seal does not constitute a product's chief value. Rather does it represent confirming testimony. The product's various proximate benefits to the user prove its relevant worth. Regarding Christ's redemptive role, preaching, teaching, and applying the ''Beatitudes'' provided the saving light and power for those who would take it. ''Anyone who hears my words and puts them into practice is like the wise man who built his house on rock.''[6] Because he had lived that way, He could die and rise as He did. The first made the second possible and valuable, hence has the same salvific impact upon humans. Only if they so live, letting the light and power obtained through apt Scriptural meditation and sacramental contemplation shine around them by serving others, will they also die and rise in Him. No alternate thorough life-insuring arrangement is available. Following that way of truth—stressing spiritual over corporeal, supernatural over natural, personally and societally, alone affords eternal life.

NOTES

1. Matt. 7:7.
2. C. de Vaux Saint-Cyr, O.P., et al. *The Sacrament of Penance* (Paramus, N.J.: Paulist Press, 1966), pp. 67–70.
3. ''The Redeemer of Man,'' Encyclical Letter of Pope John Paul II, (Boston: St. Paul Editions), p. 47. ''This sacrament [Eucharist] does for spiritual life all that material food does for the bodily life . . . by sustaining, giving increase, restoring.'' Aquinas, *Summa Theologica* Pt. III, Q.79, A.1.

4. Matt. 7:21.

5. John 10:11; "It [Christ's crucifixion] was intended to leave an example of how to follow in his footsteps."—St. Francis Assisi. Excerpt from the English translation of the office of readings from *The Liturgy of the Hours* © 1974, International Committee on English in the Liturgy, Inc. All rights reserved.

6. Matt. 7:24.

Addendum

CHRISTIAN REALITIES REGARDING PEACE

It surely is strange that so many apparently, or even officially, Christian advocates of peace give such scarce attention to what Christ said concerning this perennially pertinent topic. Obviously, His comments along those life-promoting lines were relatively few and brief. They also evidence a certain informal and occasional or spontaneous approach, which leaves them rather separated hence not so easily interpreted integrally. Both tactical techniques follow from the comparatively fundamental, prominently individualized teaching course He adopted. It aimed at making an impact upon people personally, or in their foundational features socially. The more comprehensive, collectively organized (societal) implications and applications largely remained dormant until a later time. ''I have many more things to tell you but you cannot bear it now. . . . When he (''Spirit of truth'') comes . . . he will guide you to all truth . . . he will have received from me what he will announce to you.''[1]

While the saving message thus initially conveyed was widely offered, requiring only sincere interest, the specially chosen disciples received a fuller share. Being readier respondents, those who earnestly answered the ''call,'' they became the select cadre carefully formed as official leaders of the subsequently activated

Church. "To you has been given a knowledge of the mysteries of the reign of God, but it has not been given to the others."[2] That extra understanding did not reward merely the original chosen ones. It would similarly include "those who will believe in me through their word."[3] Here we have a good example of Christ's implicit societal import. Under the Holy Spirit's further enlightening influence, the apostles eventually perceived how this sharing would occur on a duly proportioned or organically synthesized scale, naturally considered.

According with the authentic leading commission entrusted to the first followers, their like authorized successors must be recognized as holding the same official prerogatives and responsibilities. Otherwise the vitally necessary communal integrity could not continue. Different roles and corresponding duties conspicuously exist, reflecting human nature's diverse capacities. Nonetheless, an adequate substantive unity should prevail, "that all may be one, as you Father are in me, and I in you . . . that they may be one in us."[4] Additional differences, representinig relative advances toward realizing the perfecting potential inherent in the thus supernaturalized societal entity, properly characterize the membership, both general and special. These derive from degrees of dedicated acting upon the extra divine dispensation afforded through Christ's ecclesial community, bearing "a yield of a hundred, or sixty, or thirtyfold."[5]

"The others" not given that crucial knowledge regarding the kingdom were those who refused a sincere response to Christ's message. They offered "lip-service," but "hardened their hearts" against it.[6] They accepted "signs" for the corporeal benefits gained, yet ignored the word that provided spiritual meaning. The more "sophisticated" among them even propounded alleged religious reasons supposedly justifying such opposition. Contrasting the believing and unbelieving types, Christ warned, "I have come into this world to divide it, to make the sightless see and the seeing blind."[7] Human beings' historical interest in stressing subjective preferences over objective obligations underlies His seemingly self-defeating announcement: "Do not suppose that my mission on earth is to spread peace. My mission is to spread not peace, but division."[8]

Since the supernatural truth-leading way sharpens the conflict between a majority emphasizing natural autonomous assertiveness, individually and collectively, while covertly or overtly rejecting Christianity's real peacemaking capacities (personal-communal), the overall devisiveness is intensified. Radical divisions also occur within the Christian "camp" itself, consequent upon infiltrations from the secular environment. None of this should discourage Christ's really convinced followers who organically constitute the Church, however, neither personally nor communally. Their profound peace ("not as the world gives it") ought to be strengthened by the firmer faithful commitment that these challenges stimulate.

Warfare will continue around the world until the end, Christ assured us, not only politically but entailing fierce family-hostility too, and similar antagonisms at other societal levels.[9] Those dangerous adversarial relations proportionately increase as time passes and technical talents accumulate. Both apparently provide bigger and better prospects for acquisitive success when energetically employed. Although the combative confrontation seemingly may lessen periodically, and actually do so, such pauses usually promote more sophisticated modes of mutual assault. Cunningly contrived and manipulated recriminatory campaigns, as well as adroit self-adulating kinds, frequently are utilized during the interlude, to weaken opponents' wills, and "to deceive, if possible, even the elect."[10] Under these professional prevaricating conditions, public and private, Christians steadily become a resolute remnant amid the worldly-wise, consonant with Christ's additional admonition, "Because of the increase of evil, the charity of most will grow cold."[11] Lacking charity, there can be no peace, since wars represent ultimate efforts at achieving justice.

The recognition of supernatural opportunities, and apt responses to the same, arising here depend upon Christians' earnest personal and communal union in Christ. "Without me you can do nothing," His disciples were carefully warned.[12] Contrariwise, "the man who has faith in me will do the works I do and greater far than these," He told them.[13] Although doing the works that Christ did may be possible for truly committed Christians on the interpersonal plane—between individuals and informal groups, they surely cannot do greater works then. Where they may perform such greater works is at the societal, formally organized, pluralistic communal level. This constitutes the witnessing sphere left largely untouched by Christ, or approached merely marginally anyway. Organizing and operating the Church itself, besides its various relationships with similar societal agencies, comprise the greater works predicted. Not that these ecclesial officials, and their lay assistants, will so act autonomously. Rather will they serve as overt agents of Christ's covert personal presence ("I am with you always"—Matt. 28:20), activated through the Holy Spirit.

REVELATION'S SOCIETAL IMPORT

Distinguishing the personal and the communal or societal implications inherent in the Christian revelation accordingly becomes basic to its proper understanding. Those two aspects complement each other, somewhat like human development from adolescence toward adulthood, or primitive toward mature collective status. Human nature obviously follows fundamental laws while growing, or attaining gradually more thoroughly comprehensive vital conditions. Since such laws reflect the divine creative impress, the divine redemptive impact reaffirms and reinforces them. As Christ declared, "Do not think I have come to abolish the law and prophets. I have come, not to abolish them, but to fulfill them."[14]

The fulfilling supernatural import of Christ's revelatory

message for humanity on the personal score is comparatively clear, fundamentally at least. It must be expounded and extended, certainly, to cope with life's dynamic complexities; but the controlling directives can be discerned readily. Only the most elementary indicators mark the way, however, when considering its societal ramifications. The chief disciples or apostles were quite simply, if not implicitly, told that they represented a community, the Church. They similarly learned, summarily, just before their Leader left them bodily (Ascension), that its influence should be spread among all the nations. Moral norms regulating the resulting institutional relationships therefore had to be derived from the natural moral law. Aiding these efforts was a pervasive awareness of Christ's close personal presence spiritually, and the Holy Spirit's practical promptings accentuating the same.

Attempts at correlating Christ's supernatural moral standards governing personal perfection, and relevant natural moral norms regarding societal relations, show how the connections are not easily made. Although the two vital areas reciprocally characterize human nature, the latter engagements entail complications that set them apart rather radically. Involving many persons simultaneously or collectively, the ensuing joint duties and rights must be exercised through designated agents. Those public officials thus become responsible for protecting and promoting their principals' common good on a combined scale, in each societal situation. When so acting, the authorized representatives should envision the group's common concerns along personal or fundamental human lines, but secondarily, except where the values involved basically overlap. The said action consequently cannot properly include detailed personal features, reflecting more or less individualized decision and commitment, either of the leader or others. Such ancillary personal aspects correctly remain the ordinary members' province, subject to essential communal requirements. If supernatural standards are pertinent publicly, as evidently bearing upon applicable natural moral norms, ruling authorities rightly recognize and respect or apply them like the natural ones—in their common implications. Efforts at perfecting compliance with the former and the latter must be made mainly by the membership personally albeit as public obligations, accordingly fostering a due deferential autonomy. This authentically human, as reasonable or balanced, arrangement avoids mistakenly asserted extremes—identifying the personal and the communal, or opposing them. Society's respectful attitude toward moral norms, both natural and supernatural, assumes a very general form; while personal responses manifest much more specialized kinds.[15]

Every societal member shares the duties of the common good as well as its rights. Fulfilling those public obligations principally marks and practically "makes" the personal condition. Another statement by Christ implicitly confirms that natural fact, viewed supernaturally. "Whoever would preserve his life will lose it, but whoever loses his life for my sake and the gospel's will preserve it."[16] Concentrating on contributing to true communal welfare—representing humanity's God-given capacities for comprehensive development, correspondingly insures a person's individual advancement, proportionately. Through such superior faithfulness, human beings chiefly actualize their generic-specific, self-transcending or objective, really spiritual resources. In doing so, they concomitantly activate attendant particular, self-centered or subjective, corporeal counterparts. These naturally limit, temporally and spatially, the spirit's other-affirming abilities. Situations involving radical conflict between the two sectors of personal interest do arise. Conscientious Christians then resolutely maintain a balance consonant with Christ's foregoing rule regarding vital values.

Humans obviously interact along more fundamental personal lines too, as mentioned previously. This entails rather sharply particularized contacts, prominently reflecting persons' individualized aspects. Nonetheless, those limiting, separating factors properly are controlled by predominant generic-specific, spiritual or communal inclinations. Standards promoting the personal common good hold here, distinct from, and preludes to, the societal common good. Affecting comparatively elemental human relationships, the former regulating moral norms require considerably detailed practical attention. The same basic obligations apply at both living levels, societal and personal, like justice and charity, differing in degree, not kind. That is true because essentially the same reciprocal substantive connection—spiritual dominating corporeal, prevails on the two complementary social planes. Persons mutually engage one another, albeit under different responsible conditions therefore, either individually or collectively constituted.[17]

As also noted earlier, generic-specific, objective components control particular subjective ones very thoroughly when the second situation exists. They exercise such self-transcending influence only somewhat marginally amid the first set of circumstances. This decisive difference follows upon a correspondingly increased profundity and complexity (combined) characterizing the societal enterprise. These necessitate proportionately fuller analytic considerations, preparing for the firmer moral commitments demanded. Thus, determining justice's and charity's concrete content where communal duties apply, involves confronting human conditions vastly magnified beyond the sort pertaining to immediate interpersonal relations. The respective common goods certainly are not congruent, neither naturally nor supernaturally. Christ clearly recognized those vitally important distinctions. The charitable practices propounded by Him—turning the other cheek, giving shirt along with cloak, going an extra mile—represented individual personal responses in quite minor offending injustices. He definitely did not recommend the same reaction toward very serious personal wrongdoing however. Under such scandalous circumstances, when the common societal, hence likewise the more individually transcendent, collectively shared personal, good was drastically damaged, He advocated forceful defensive measures instead. "What terrible things will come on the world through scandal!. . . . Woe to the man through whom scandal comes. . . . It would be better for anyone who leads astray . . . (a "little one"—scandal of the weak) to be drowned . . . in the depths of the sea."[18]

Implicit here is the moral principle that society may justly defend its crucial values by imposing capital punishment upon whoever assault them; and so threaten the members' spiritual welfare even more than the corporeal. Responsible officials obviously must exercise reasonable restraint, justly and charitably, naturally and supernaturally; but the supreme sanction can be utilized to protect the community. The offender benefits from the penalty too, if rightly accepted, accordingly making radical amends for the crime and becoming spiritually renewed. Society's members share this obligation of defending the public common good, within their proper unofficial scope. Then we have a situation where the individual personal common good and the societal counterpart merge, as mentioned before. Whenever they do, individual discretion or toleration toward evil no longer holds. The community's more thoroughly personal, fuller spiritual (generic-specific) aspects preempts the offending agents' more marginally personal, less spiritual (particularized) features. Otherwise charity falsely contradicts justice, rather than correctly completing it. Christ's example regarding one's radical separation from any who refuse the Church's judgment against offensive conduct illustrates the fundamental principle.[19]

REVELATION'S IMPORT FOR DEFENSIVE WAR

An additional basically pertinent societal fact was acknowledged by Christ: "Give to Caesar what is Caesar's, but give to God what is God's."[20] Civil society has legitimate official leaders, whose reasonable directives the members should obey. That legitimacy is founded on two crucial factors, or naturally and supernaturally viewed. The latter received explicit emphasis in His statement to Pilate: "You would have no power over me whatever, unless it were given from above."[21] Civil authority ultimately represents divine authority therefore. The natural support entails human elements, duly representing the citizens' needs and interests. Both responsibilities are fulfilled through appropriate endeavors promoting the societal common good.

Christ similarly stressed another more immediately relevant social or interpersonal fact, which, like the foregoing option for capital punishment, recognized prudent natural defensive measures under humanity's unstable peaceful conditions. "When a strong man fully armed guards his courtyard, his possessions go undisturbed. But when someone stronger than he comes and overpowers him, such a one carries off the arms on which he was relying and divides the spoils."[22] Contextually considered, the admonition apparently agrees with His customary teaching approach—setting standards properly governing individualized personal relations. So far as it does apply at this comparatively informal social level, the norm differs very noticeably from similar interpersonal principles announced during "the Sermon on the Mount." Christ drew no distinction here between the naturally accepted practice and a higher supernatural alternative, as on the other (mount) occasion. Evidently, then, such approval reflects the more serious situation involved, and consequently the propriety of active defense (proportionate preparedness anyway) against potential aggressors. That sharply forceful attitude complements the one concerning preferable penalties accorded scandalizers, as noted above.

Although these authorized resorts to defensive force are declared by Christ in His usual individually personalized manner, He hardly could have intended them for explicit implementation directly. So employed, they would adversely affect, if not almost entirely offset, other fundamental reforming efforts channelled through Him. Both really represent implicit intimations regarding critical societal responsibilities. Public officials must maintain resources that will adequately protect their citizens from internal and external marauders. Admittedly, the circumstances surrounding and stimulating Christ's distinctively punitive statements point mainly toward moral and spiritual arming, on the second count especially. Nonetheless, corporeal counterparts clearly have correspondingly pronounced significance, consonant with human nature's essentially consolidated condition. This combined interpretation is further confirmed by His testimony before Pilate: "If my kingdom were of this world, my subjects would be fighting to save me from being handed over to the Jews."[23]

Additional elemental or individualized personal injunctions support Christ's recommendations entailing forceful defensive action. The redemptive mission's central reformative meaning was summarily, if inferentially, stated when He explained how, "It is the spirit that gives life, the flesh is useless."[24] Reasserting and retaining that long compromised yet crucially controlling personal balance constitutes the prime requisite promoting humans' saving "rebirth." Only then can they consciously relate to God as spirit, and so progressively attain eternal life. Only then can they find and follow the way insuring such a fulfilling relationship. The said mediating essential vital fact comprises the telling truth organically synthesizing Christ's consummating revelatory role, as "the way, the truth, and the life." It therefore affords an acceptor the key unlocking the mystery of His messianic message's invigorating import.

Thus, what made possible the apostles' "knowledge of the mysteries of the reign of God" was their spiritual ardor. "The others" were not "given" it because they had become blinded by fleshy fancies. What makes the overall difference between the "sightless" who "see," and the "seers" who are "blind," is the firsts' spiritual inclination and the seconds' corporeal concentration. This decisive incongruity substantively likewise accounts for the drastic divisions disrupting familial and similar societal institutions. It also chiefly causes evil's calamitous increase over the centuries, with a proportionate chilling effect upon charity. Contrarily, those who save their lives while "losing" them accomplish that astounding result through spiritual sublimation, as Christ explicitly demonstrated. The same dominant spiritual conviction and commitment facilitates one's faith in His truly liberating challenge: "Do not worry about those who deprive the body of life but cannot destroy the soul . . . fear him who can destroy both body and soul in Gehenna."[25] Such supernaturalized spiritual awareness, aptly adjusted concretely to a superior appreciation of the common good's divine reflection, and its attendant, personally enhancing objective obligation, encourages the sincere Christian toward laying down his or her life for friends, when necessary.[26] The total self-denying (subjectively-individually), other-avowing (objectively-personally) process is symbolized by the cross. This represents the way, in truth, to eternal life, on a steadily advancing personal scale.

Among real Christians, then, spiritual values decisively dominate corporeal kinds. The balance holds both at the more elemental, individual personal level, and the more comprehensive communal or societal one. They understand how consistent theoretical and practical dedication along these interiorly inspired lines alone insures full personal or thorough human development. They likewise recognize that their basically weakened natural condition, which follows from an original, prototypical, personal default, regularly requires extra efforts of a supernatural sort. This means witnessing publicly, besides privately, so others "may see your good works"; thus "bringing forth fruit" by doing "the will of the Father." Without the former, the latter becomes merely mechanical self-indulgence. With it, however, those others will be encouraged, perhaps initially inspired, towards looking and living beyond corporeally confining values. Where war, or its possibilities, is an issue, the public emphasis upon proper personal balance, spiritual over corporeal, should increase.

TRANSTEMPORARY OVER CONTEMPORARY BALANCE

As we have seen, Christ implicitly approved apt public preparedness to defend the societal common good from potential and
actual enemies. By implication also, He approved appropriate
use of such resources, human and physical, for defensive purposes. Correctly considered, naturally-supernaturally, the common values endangered are principally spiritual, supplementally
corporeal; jointly but deferentially promoting true human development. A society's real enemies consequently manifest themselves mainly in their activities against its vital spirit, directly,
and/or indirectly through concentrated attacks on its bodily welfare. If these assaults reach a serious scale, drastically damaging
the collective integrity, thus concertedly interpreted, proportionate spiritual-corporeal force may be employed protectively. The
relevant valid defensive measures adopt the punitive practices
traditionally termed "capital punishment," when checking chiefly
internal, individually initiated offenses; and limited lethal war,
when combatting external, politically organized opponents. Just-
war standards have been formulated, under the Church's auspices,
further elucidating the foregoing fundamental, natural-supernatural, societal moral norms that Christ affirmed. By so authoritively and interpretively acting, the Church specifically exemplifies
its Founder's prediction, namely, that His followers would do
greater things than He. As we saw before too, this entails extending the relatively elemental individual-personal moral norms
received from Him to the more comprehensive societal-personal
level.

Like other moral principles governing human living, those
bearing upon just warfare must allow for changing conditions
significantly affecting their theoretical expression, as well as concrete interpretation and practical application. While the basic,
transtemporary features of the human agents involved remain

constant, consonant with a substantial spiritual content, certain variations in contemporary relevance occur, reflecting continuing creaturely development. Such alterations are influenced largely by tangible temporal, prominently quantitive, corporeal factors; yet simultaneously represent some adjustments (additive mainly) on predominantly qualitive, permanent spiritual counts. The former must be kept under the latter's control, if progress would be promoted, thus emulating Christ's example, fulfilling the natural law. A typical critical contemporary problem confronted here derives from the tremendously destructive nuclear power now pertinent to defensive war.

High among important facts deserving close consideration on that score is the very evident realistic attitude that Christ's statement regarding vigilant defensive preparedness manifests. Human history has shown how firm bargaining, or battling if necessary, positions help greatly toward restraining undue assertiveness by aggressive expansionists. The credible capacity for imposing potent penalties upon opponents who might become assailants more often than not exerts a corresponding chilling and checking effect. This deterring impact usually works better amid societal or collective relations than the interpersonal kind, since punitive consequences are less easily escaped en masse. Accordingly, we have another natural confirmation of Christ's favorable comments upon adequate arming as being concerned mainly with public policy. True, such forceful readiness in itself does not insure peace between societies or individuals, and occasionally terrible confrontations have erupted. The said alert stance reflects merely a somewhat negative, "stop-grab" attitude at best; hence requires additional positive promotional assistance, along reasonable compromising lines, if the overall outcome would be mutually beneficial, realistically viewed. Compromise also has proper limits that must receive even firmer respect. Christ's warning against sacrificing the spirit while protecting the body establishes the crucial boundary or balance correctly controlling reason. Public officials' responsibility for the societal common good, essentially spiritual-moral values and norms predominantly, obligates them not to subvert these through excessive corporeal emphasis (rationalization).

Societal leaders similarly should avoid an alternate extreme of spiritual subversion, involving uninhibited threats or attacks by nuclear weapons. Disproportionate, dominantly corporeally contrived, thus chiefly destructive, defensive measures likewise are morally reprehensible, as the just-war doctrine specifically declares. The telling question regarding what physical power is permissible and what not so only can be answered rightly with apt insights into proportionality's import. This means maintaining a truly reasonable correlation between the defending position—retaliatory instruments' punishing capacities as stocked and stationed, and the good effects expected from their employment, again realistically envisioned. As we observed previously, safeguarding the societal common good represents the principal benefit for consideration. That was seen as demanding due concentration on the members' spiritual advancement over accompanying deferentially supplemental corporeal improvements. Recognizing the profound disparity characterizing them, despite an essential mutuality, and also the ultimate advantages gained through the latters' radical subjection to the former (even total sacrifice temporally), the societal common good may concretely require an accentuated adoption of such a definitely disciplined personal and communal stand.

The ensuing sharply increased corporeal risks should simultaneously intensify the affected society's spiritual consciousness and commitment, correspondingly enhancing its individual participants' personal good proportionately. Similar sublimating opportunities would devolve upon the opposing society's membership, as well as other more or less significantly implicated neighboring societies' population. Living under these tangibly threatening conditions can help people become influenced better by transtemporary, or supernatural eternal, values, rather than contemporary, natural contingent kinds. This general spiritual mobilization should suit Christians especially, aiding a closer conformance with the vigilance Christ stressed concerning His promised return. Then they enjoy regular reminders regarding the warning He issued against current careless attitudes toward that apocalyptic event: "As it was in the days of Noah (and Lot) so will it be in the days of the Son of Man . . . they ate and drank they took husbands and wives . . . they bought and sold, they built and planted . . . whoever tries to preserve his life will lose it. . . ."[27] Likewise, if humans' vaunted cultural accomplishments tempts (temporizes) them to join in the popular and professional rationalization of their permanence, Christ's additional admonition should lessen that secular enthusiasm. "What man thinks important God holds in contempt (contemporary)."[28] Although Christians must earnestly work at promoting the good or godly actualities and potentialities that civilizing cultures possess, they understand how those apt advances yet must experience a radical transformation, through creation's cataclysmic climax when time ends.

While all is being said and done, then, toward preserving peace between profoundly different societies, by reasonable compromise within proper spiritually controlling limits, a society so rationally ordered still rightly may maintain military efficiency adequate for protection from possible physical assault, realistically considered. Where such preparedness includes utilizing nuclear defensive systems, may this society morally activate these systems against a similarly armed and attacking enemy?

DEFENSIVE USE OF NUCLEAR WEAPONS

The problem here reflects the fact that widespread damage, entailing innumerable innocent human casualties, will certainly occur. The latter would be true, at least, if the nuclear weapons were employed on a major scale. Limited, localized usage upon military targets, strictly defined and confined, does not involve the same destructive danger, directly anyway. Obviously, though, even restricted tactical commitment could easily expand into much larger lethal dimensions. Nonetheless, our foregoing appraisal of Christ's approving position concerning proportionate defensive arrangements, with its societal implications and ramifications, as further explicated by the just war doctrine, evidently does justify a reasonable tactical nuclear approach. Both supporting sources similarly impose correspondingly increased obligations regarding the reasonable element, under those enormously endangering conditions. They surely stress such duty much more, whenever societal officials set about determining whether or not strategic nuclear defenses may be activated.

The first factor for reasonable recognition here is the practical truth, that a society having the moral right to maintain arms matching realistically predictable defensive needs likewise has the concomitant right to use them, when concrete circumstances really require it. Admitting the first, but not the second claim in effect countenances fraud or hypocrisy. Christ certainly never would recommend this duplicity. The said society may decide against exercising the right, yet still holds the same. A second pertinent factor bears upon the proportionality between good and evil consequences following from the allowed action. While supplemental corporeal and material components are very relevant, as potential items of loss, they have much less vital value than their spiritual counterparts. Christ clearly confirmed such a fundamental natural fact at the elementary personal human level. His official ecclesial representatives subsequently show its significance on the more comprehensive societal plane.

We noted earlier how the societal common good, extending or enhancing the personal kind, chiefly comprises spiritual values. These accordingly constitute the goods that everty society mainly must protect and promote, though not unduly neglecting corporeal supplements. Additionally, those protective and promotive endeavors should include the larger common good embracing other organically affected societies. Therefore, if a nuclear assault that subverts spiritual values beneath corporeal ones threatens any society's true common good, adequately viewed, it may utilize strategic nuclear weapons reasonably to defend itself. The resultant spiritual gains, achieved through a morally inspired, carefully conducted defensive action, offset accompanying corporeal loss.

Reasonable standards applicable then are expressed in the just-war theory. However, the traditional statements must be understood and interpreted along more thoroughly Christian lines. This means correlating them better with the biblical pronouncements of Christ. The principal clarification concerns human life's import. Such a consolidated concept ought no longer be employed simplistically, thus allowing an excessive corporeal emphasis. Instead, its transtemporary spiritual content should receive accentuated affirmation. The same improvement holds for pertinent papal and conciliar declarations. Then Christ's stress upon the spirit's crucial transtemporary vital value is afforded due respect, and a properly decisive dominion over the contemporary corporeal component explicitly recognized. That essential distinction between greater and lesser goods characterizing human nature intrinsically, provides permanent objective conditions justifying radical discriminating actions. Under extreme circumstances, the inferior corporeal element rightly can be sacrificed entirely, while protecting, if not promoting, superior spiritual resources proportionately.

Apt sacrificial action requires careful consideration on the performers' part, to insure an integral profitable balance—among those who make the critical move, those significantly affected by it, and those in whose behalf it is initiated. Besides being strictly defensive, and principally protecting against spiritual subversion, the said saving activity must restrain destructive effects as much as possible. Corporeal and physical damage may be tolerated, but never chiefly advocated or propagated. Defending efforts with nuclear weapons, otherwise permitted as explained above, still should refrain from unnecessary harmful consequences. This entails conscientious endeavors at maintaining meaningful control, like planning gradual nuclear strikes involving mainly military objectives, even though the resulting destruction inevitably will extend beyond the targeted boundaries. Demanding more restriction than that is unreasonable, as excessively constrained corporeally.

Such a responsible systematic approach, similarly implemented, insures a spiritually disciplined attitude in the defending society's relevant public agencies. Disseminating accurate information regarding the plan to the total membership, emphasizing especially its spiritual-moral contours, facilitates the latter's acceptance and personal adjustment. Thus further alerted concerning their obligations toward the societal common good, under exceptionally trying circumstances, the members have corresponding opportunities for cultivating an intensified spiritual commitment. There may be little the defenders can do positively by way of aiding the attacker's population through advance warnings, since those communications ordinarily are severely curtailed. Due care while activating counter-battery would constitute a certain positive assistance indirectly. Somewhat identical deficiencies mar the help afforded societies rather marginally yet still seriously affected. These very evident precautionary weaknesses, as well as the kind implicit in the nuclear combative process, should remind religious people, Christians above all others, that human destiny remains dependent upon God more than mankind. Transcending popular and pseudoscientific or idealistic claims directing attention solely toward despairing corporeal and physical projections, deriving from strictly naturalistic conceptions, they should proportionately encourage the fearful against worldly-wise prognostications. This means sharing their strengthening supernatural convictions regarding divine Providence's constant saving support, even amid calamities, which fosters hope. As Christ advised, ''Do not live in fear. . . . It has pleased your Father to give you the kingdom.''[29] To societies that ''Seek out . . . his kingship over you,'' through earnest efforts at protecting and promoting transtemporary spiritual-moral values, despite contemporary corporeal costs, ''the rest (including profound if not entire peace) will follow in turn.''[30]

NOTES

1. John 16:12–14.
2. Matt. 13:11.
3. John 17:30.
4. Ibid., v.31.
5. Matt. 13:23.
6. Ibid., 15:8; John 8:43.
7. John 9:39.
8. Matt. 10:34–36; Mark 13:12–13.
9. Ibid.
10. Mark 13:23.
11. Matt. 24:12; Luke 18:8, ''When the Son of Man comes, will he find any faith on earth?''
12. John 15:5.
13. Ibid., 14:12.
14. Matt. 5:17.
15. Aquinas, *Summa Theologica*, II–II, Q.58, A.7.
16. Mark 8:35.
17. Aquinas, *Summa Theologica*, Q.58, A.5.
18. Matt. 18:6–7. Cf. Mark 9:42.
19. Matt. 18:17.
20. Mark 12:17.
21. John 19:11.
22. Luke 11:21.
23. John 18:36.
24. Ibid., 6:63.
25. Matt. 10:28.
26. John 15:13.
27. Luke 17:26–33.
28. Ibid., 16:15.
29. Luke 12:32.
30. Ibid., 31.

Second Addendum

CHRISTIAN CULTURAL AND FAMILIAL ROLES

Commenting upon the theological enterprise, especially its moral aspects, the second Vatican Council advised theologians that "its scientific expositions should be more thoroughly nourished by scriptural teaching."[1] This advice is consistent with the Council's more elementary explanation contained in statements concerning divine revelation.

> Sacred theology rests on the written Word of God, together with sacred tradition, as its primary and perpetual foundation. By scrutinizing in the light of faith all truth stored up in the mystery of Christ, theology is most powerfully strengthened and constantly rejuvenated by that Word. For the sacred Scriptures contain the Word of God . . . and so the study of the sacred page is, as it were, the soul of sacred theology.[2]

The Council also notes how ". . . among all the Scriptures, even those of the New Testament, the Gospels have a special preeminence . . . for they are the principal witness for the life and teaching of . . . our Saviour."[3] "Besides the four Gospels," we are then told, "the canon of the New Testament also contains the epistles of St. Paul and other apostolic writings, . . . by which . . . (Christ's) true teaching is more and more fully stated."[4] Such fuller stating of Christ's true teaching entails a continuous development, the Council reminds us. "For as the centuries succeed one another, the Church constantly moves forward toward the fulness of divine truth until the words of God reach their complete fulfillment in her."[5] Christ's own announcement on the latter point has prime significance here: "I have much more to tell you, but you cannot bear it now. When he comes, however, being the Spirit of truth (Paraclete) he will guide you to all truth . . . he will have received from me what he will announce to you."[6]

Giving closer consideration to Scripture accordingly facilitates progress in better understanding Christ's saving message. However, like any other humanly related or affected good, some serious problems can confront its users. Among the more easily evident types are those that stem from the Scriptural resource's extensive and intensive content. Besides the plentiful and most meaningful testimony by Christ Himself, we have the numerous interpretations and applications that His official followers supply. Consequently, when utilizing such varied profound references, a certain selectivity always is necessary. Human limitations obviously prevent a fully complete coverage under any given searching conditions. Responsible researchers must be diligently careful, therefore, regarding selections made as support for their theological statements. At the least they should insure a truly reasonable, or more than less, consistency between the special extraction's immediate import, and the sacred source's general implications concerning the pertinent theme. Another complicating factor requires close attention. Since Scripture—even if viewed only as New Testament, the present study's position—reflects different authors' or speakers' stands, due emphasis upon relative continuity (mainly with Christ's own actions) cannot be exaggerated.

The first of these two connected complications represents this study's critical target. Stated more exactly, the ensuing examinations and corresponding explanations will stress a persistent relevant negative attitude toward Christ's teachings, apropos of the family's supernatural significance, in the Church's doctrinal pronouncements. Concomitantly, the study will offer evidence indicating, implicitly anyway, cultural combinations' proper supernatural superiority within the Christian dispensation. The said superiority is seen as a fundamental or essential societal one; hence it does not automatically include all concretely existing examples. Recognizing modern secularized societal excesses, where spiritual values are compromised and subverted through an extreme dedication to otherwise legitimate corporeal interests, families frequently must exercise their duly proportionate supernatural responsibility, besides a similar natural one, combatting cultural secularism.

TYPICAL TEACHINGS OF THE CHURCH ON THE FAMILY

Because the Church's moral-spiritual teachings are founded upon permanently enduring natural and supernatural principles or realities, current expressions ever manifest a continuous tradition. Accordingly, our subsequent analysis shall highlight recent official statements as examples. Along like introductory explaining lines, mention also should be made here how our focal considerations will point out merely those declarations that have a direct connection with Christ's pertinent affirmations. What was said previously regarding the study's objectives makes this analytic arrangement rather a foregone conclusion.

Selections from the second Vatican Council's pronouncements concerning marriage and the family provide apt opening references. The Council restates the Church's traditional doctrine emphasizing marriage's sacramental character. It cites Christ's comment summarizing the relationship's essential meaning: "no longer two but one flesh" (Matt. 19:6).[7] The only other relevant assertion of Christ that the Council supplies is the quite oblique one about the "groom's" personal impact on fasting by "wedding guests" (Matt. 9:15, Mark 2:19–20, Luke, 5:34–35).[8] The Council refers to Pope Pius XI's encyclical, *Casti Connubii,* several times. He presents three quotes significant for our purposes. In the first one, Christ recalls a woman's joy after successfully completing pregnancy (John 16:21). The second warns against lustful looking at women, as constituting adultery (Mark 5:28). A third stresses neighborly service, as comprising the controlling standard at the Last Judgment (Matthew 25:34ff).[9]

Pope Paul VI's encyclical, *Humanae Vitae,* lists five statements of Christ. They actually bear upon familial relations merely marginally. He cites the final apostolic commission, "teach all nations" (Matt. 28:18–19). Then comes the reminder about fulfilling God's will and its critical import for salvation (Matt. 7:21).[10] Next we are turned toward the admonition regarding the yoke of Christ being sweet (Matt. 11:30). A fourth reference contains the ultimate urgent challenge: "the gate is narrow and the way is hard that leads to life" (Matt. 7:14).[11] The final pertinent scriptural connection underscores Christ's saving rather than condemning role (John 3:17).[12]

Pope John Paul II's lengthy exhortation, "The Community of the Family," likewise is sparse on links with Christ's comments, beyond those affecting the family fundamentally. He includes the usual explanation concerning marriage's natural beginning (Matt. 19:5).[13] The basic "two in one flesh" norm receives customary attention, and also the traditional opposition to divorce (Matt. 19:6).[14] Christ's culminating prayer, "that they may be one," gets passing notice, omitting the crucial modifying or vitally determining part, "as you Father in me and I in you" (John 17:21).[15] A similar brief extract from the "little children's" parable avoids the accompanying dynamically distinguishing element involved there: "whoever does not accept the kingdom of God as a child (in faith) will not enter into it" (Luke 18:16; Matt. 19:14; Mark 10:15).[16] Lacking such decisive distinction, mature

Christian living in hope and charity becomes impossible. Again stressing the minimal somewhat, the Pope acclaims Christ's negative praise for those who give handy help (cup of cold water) "to one of these little ones" (Matt. 10:42).[17] Shifting toward the opposite practical extreme, John Paul emphasizes the universal evangelizing command, "preach the Gospel to the whole creation" (Mark 16–15).[18] Facilely fitting both extremities together, thus achieving another striking simplification, he very easily identifies Christ's overall ecclesial commendation ("where two or three are gathered . . . I am in their midst") with the family on an especially significant scale (Matt. 18:19–20).[19]

CHRIST'S TEACHINGS CONCERNING THE FAMILY

Quite early during His earthly life, Christ displayed a decidedly detached attitude regarding familial ties. The incident showing Him taking leave of His parents while visiting the distant temple, unannounced previously and over several days, when only twelve, surely manifests much independence. As the sharply nonapologetic response He offered upon being questioned about the absence's meaning demonstrates, profoundly superior obligations eclipsed domestic duties even at that tender age (Luke 2:45–50). Higher religious spiritual responsibilities radically outranked lower parental, more corporeal kinds, despite His definitely adolescent status.

The initial trans-parent social approach received still fuller confirmation and extension throughout Christ's subsequent saving mission. The latter entailed merely three years devoted to mature public service, after some thirty years spent amid the family. Although undoubtedly exerting a real influence on His later activity, the household's effects principally were elementary, hence all but completely unmentioned in the crucial social teachings and practices. Where He did give moral advice apropos of familial relations, those declarations clearly inclined toward deflating seemingly normal domestic connections, while proportionately exalting fuller concentrated interpersonal counterparts.

Allowing for scriptural reporting condensations, Christ's direct calling or recruiting methods reflected little involvement with parental reactions. Such a trans-parent attitude was exhibited very prominently by His abrupt answer when a potential disciple requested leave that would permit a parent's burial: "Let the dead bury their dead; follow me" (Matt. 8:21–22). Another ready recruit earned a similar sharp rebuke after asking an apparently brief delay to bid parents farewell: "Whoever puts his hand to the plow and looks back is not worthy of the kingdom" (Luke 9:62). Yet more severely, some were told: "If anyone comes to me without turning his back on his father and mother, his wife and children, his brothers and sisters . . . he cannot be my follower" (Luke 14:26). This drastic initial downgrading of kinship's loyalties represented Christ's consistent overall social impact. As He explained quite starkly, "I have come to set a man at odds with his father, a daughter with her mother . . . : in short, to make a man's enemies those of his own household" (Matt. 10:35–36). Enmity would frequently exist there through serious conflicts concerning efforts at following Christ's witnessing example. Whoever adopts His fully committed course must remember that "no prophet is without honor except in his native place and in his own house" (Matt. 13:57). Consequently, Christ's followers should heighten and broaden standards governing kinship like their Leader, for Whom "whoever does the will of my heavenly Father is brother and sister and mother to me" (Matt. 12:48–50). Though that supernaturalized personal attitude will entail much hardship, it affords corresponding benefits. On Christ's own testimony, "everyone who gives up home, brothers, sisters, father or mother, wife or children . . . for my sake will receive many times as much and inherit eternal life" (Matt. 19:29).

The main reason behind these admonitions loosening the family's natural bonds derives from the crucial reforming injunction that Christ issued: "It is the spirit that gives life; the flesh is useless. The words I spoke to you are spirit and life" (John 6:63). Since the marital relationship underlying and proximately producing the family is a prominently fleshly one ("two in one flesh"), albeit aptly spiritually controlled, the latter especially reflects such tangible influences. While naturally a most important societal unit, as initially forming (generating and educating) society's members, its role there remains quite limited. A pervasive localized, temporalized outlook characterizes those connections. Measured against the Christian dispensation's supernaturally charged vital values, the family's personal and communal or societal limitations become still more evident. Despite the extra sacramental assistance provided, thus really preventing the spouses sinking into fleshly individualistic extremes nearly equal with their actually rising above them, domestic living inherently tends toward restrictive results. It thus rather resembles the body's impact upon the spirit, personally and proximately, but also communally somewhat remotely. Because Christ's chiefly reforming mission required a radically increased stress on spirit over body, He necessarily had to accentuate a proportionately balanced personal-spiritual liberating advance beyond strongly individual-corporeal confining familial ties. "Flesh begets flesh; spirit begets spirit," He said.[20]

SOME TRADITIONAL INCOMPLETENESS IN THE CHURCH'S TEACHING ON THE FAMILY

The Church's traditional praise of the family as the primordial societal unit certainly is correct. However, the supernatural handicaps inherent there seldom are mentioned. St. Paul tells us, ". . . the spirtual was not first; first came the natural and after that the spiritual. . . ."[21] Accordingly, from a truly Christian viewpoint, being first among the essential societal institutions carries less meaning than coming later. The heavenly kingdom's

evolutionary advance involved much intensive and extensive preliminary preparation, humanly considered. Subsequent innate or
essential improvements in the human system comprise fuller constitutional developments naturally. They similarly facilitate richer
supernatural manifestations substantively and dynamically. The
long period preceding Christ's first coming after the original
creation indicates such needed prior expansions. The Church's
own autonomous existence exemplifies those historical facts. It
reflects extended earlier efforts at establishing religious agencies'
independence alongside parallel political authority, as that maturing process was supernaturally sublimated through Christ's
directly divine intervention.[22] So, too, does the Church's official
moral-spiritual teaching, wherein the natural law's basic human
directives become clarified and consolidated further under Revelation's supernaturally enlightening influence.[23]

The latter enhancing contributions represent Christ's continuing completing effect on the natural law as He promised.[24] When
making these additional interpretations and applications, though,
it surely is not enough to expand largely along the said natural
lines, merely suplemented by fundamental, loosely abstract correlations with some very general statements or elemental mystical
implications of Christ. This artificial approach promotes superficially glorified results, which make the family appear as the
principal societal unit besides the ecclesial entity (so-called
Church in little). If we would emphasize the domestic institution's
Christian role correctly, or adequately, the credits given it should
be thoroughly realistic. That requires recognizing and respecting
the pertinent personal and societal limitations pertaining thereto,
thus appropriately emulating and extending Christ's example.

St. Paul's primitive reference to the Church as ''the bride
of Christ'' (Eph. 5:22–32) and his insistence upon identifying
this interpretation with Christian matrimony for mutually reinforcing purposes provide a telling concrete sample. Employing
such elemental symbolism risks having the Church reflect on its
vital significance in excessively minute, tangible, technical or

extremely quantitive terms. When one utilizes those highly abstract notions, their practical ramifications entail the widest and least restrained imaginative indulgences. Contrariwise, and perhaps more pertinently, the said analogue's very abstruseness may incline many toward avoiding the idea altogether, except under the most pressing circumstances. Stressing the concept's personal marital import further facilitates a somewhat exorbitant imagery. The Church's overall sacramental status is then too often envisioned along easygoing, staidly settled, household lines, rather than the truly challenging, "light of the world," "salt of the earth" kind which Christ actually gave it. Besides that relative reductionism regarding the ecclesial institution itself, the stated image must affect the married partners not a little extravagantly. If they take it seriously at all, they hardly can escape assuming a vaguely mechanical, comparatively angelic attitude. Some valuable benefits obviously accrue (promoting permanence), but scarcely the sort fostering realistic or reasonable, aptly balanced human living.

While respecting St. Paul's early profoundly relevant insight, the limitations attached thereto greatly diminish any usefulness in later days. The Church's increasingly comprehensive self-understanding, including corresponding connections with the world, makes Christ's own relational reference the better one for contemporary conditions. Proper emphasis upon interpersonal relations as a whole, so much a critical issue of our time, recommends using His imagery: ". . . that all may be one as you, Father, are in me, and I in you. . . ."[25] Correctly understood, the union involved there represents a thoroughly personal, truly spiritual or communal type, as against the more marginal spiritual-corporeal blending in the bridal image. The said personal-communal implications reflect not only all informal, largely individualized, social contacts, but likewise all formal, fuller personal, societal-communal relationships. Familial bonds are contained implicitly, being one systematized collective unit among others humanly refracting the divine personal-communal union. A firmly objective, proportionately balanced or reasonable standard thus results, both permitting and requiring a vastly enhanced accuracy amid extended explanations and applications.

As we observed previously, Christ consistently devalued the family's personal import, although duly acknowledging its fundamental relevance, throughout His earthly mission. That reforming action's crucial meaning probably is succinctly indicated by correlating two statements pertinent here. One has been mentioned already ("Flesh begets flesh; spirit begets spirit"). The other was made at the same time: "No one can see the reign of God unless he is begotten from above."[26] Surely the family shares the supernatural blessings of this rebirth through its sacramental significance (fulfilling matrimony). Those benefits are proportioned to the recipients' natural capacities, however, consonant with human nature's essential requirements on the whole. At the individual-personal level, the body participates in supernatural life, as natural, derivatively, through the soul's intrinsic complementing union. The latter principally experiences the exalting effects.[27] Similarly, at the societal-communal level, the family enjoys supernatural advantages rather vicariously, or chiefly by an involvement in other more inherently spiritual human combinations. The primary example there follows from the Church's impact upon the domestic agency. Adequately considered, though, the family has an even closer collective ally, namely, the cultural institution, as we shall see subsequently. It essentially parallels the former proximately, hence correspondingly enriches that societal counterpart spiritually, when both respect the Church's properly prior elucidations of Christ's teachings.

FULLER FUNDAMENTAL FEATURES OF CHRIST'S TEACHINGS

We have seen how the crucial factor for Christ's characteristic reforming role in His emphasis on the need to reassert human nature's correct personal balance (spiritual over corporeal).

Everything else He said and did more or less reflected such pivotal constitutional truth. The principle accordingly represents the central theme consolidating His total truth which "will make you free."[28] It opens real connections with God, Who "is Spirit."[29] It also supplies the key unlocking the human mystery, like the cosmic order as a whole. Besides this elementary substantive enlightenment, Christ's critical vital truth provides the typical mediating component linking the forces comprising humanity's essential developmental dynamism. He summarized the messianic mission's meaning there when declaring, "I am the way, and the truth, and the life. . . . "[30] Thus we have succinctly stated supernaturally, the progressive process (methods, means, ends) whereby human beings, as all creatures, attain fulfillment. Under the given guiding conditions, or applied to humans, the middle creaturely class between higher angelic and lower physical-biological extremities,[31] the truth or means vector holds the main value.[32] Only through a ready and steady stress there, principally refracting spirit's dominant impress upon body, can human agents maintain an effective balance regarding the fulfilling life or ends available, and the practically pertinent ways or methods promoting the same.

Life thus constitutes the ultimately controlling, theoretical priciple for human beings, with the way entailing the proximately determining, practical principle. Neither is really understandable, much less overtly actionable aptly, severally or jointly, unless interpreted and correlated correctly by means of the mediate, combined theoretical-practical principle—truth. Truth consequently intertwines and invigorates life and its way, mainly through the enlightening and empowering insights deriving from its basic substantial structural core—spiritual dominating corporeal. Life, as well as the way, will have humanly relevant significance only if so crucially substantiated and consolidated via that truth. Christ's emphasis upon the cross's decisive importance—denying the subjective, comparatively more corporeal self, while affirming the objective, proportionately more spiritual other (even accepting complete corporeal demise)—confirms such vital, truthful order. His own eventual death, resurrection, and glorification thoroughly completes it.

Although Christ's foregoing natural and supernatural revelations primarily or explicitly influence personal-individual human relations, they implicitly affect societal-communal affairs. As the Church teaches, the latter represent more comprehensive extensions to the fundamental human potential.[33] Christ indirectly indicated this when He told the disciples, ". . . the man who has faith in me will do the works I do, and greater far than these. . . ."[34] Since He had earlier said, "no student is greater than his teacher . . . ,"[35] the greater works they will do evidently involve socially organized services, which He had left for their later initiative, under His continuing inspiration (with the Holy Spirit) through the officially commissioned Church.

The Church's historical development as the principal supernatural societal entity, rightly exercising a superior salvific impact upon related collective agencies, has followed a discernable dynamic pattern. As the second Vatican Council explains, those communal connections entail mutually beneficial progressive exchanges in the chief societal sectors that have evolved naturally. They are political, cultural, familial, and economic.[36] When we examine the characteristic communal units closely alongside the Church, more typically reflecting the corresponding religious sector, we find a constitutional and dynamic vital order very much like the personal-individual one. Thus, at the overall purposeful, goal-setting or guiding societal level, two parallel, distinct, proportionately correlated communal spheres exist: the religious and the political. Such a distinguishable, but not properly separable, relationship manifests human nature's spiritual-corporeal counterparts, projected collectively. As on the personal-individual plane, the former should exert a due suzerainty over the latter, naturally and still more so supernaturally.

Viewed from the opposite dynamic extremity—procedural, methods-serving, or sharply activating sector—within the total societal framework, we observe another constitutionally contrasting yet essentially complementary combination. There, society's fine arts and mundane arts or economic processes incessantly interact, as mutually assisting spiritual and corporeal forces respectively (if correctly constructed). Arranged between the two activating alternatives (the guiding purposeful and the overtly activating procedural), hence supporting and synthesizing them, severally and jointly, are the two respectively spiritual and corporeal communal divisions: cultural and familial. They proportionately provide means-forming or structuring services for the other collective types, while correspondingly integrating themselves along duly deferential constitutional lines, spiritual over corporeal.

THE CULTURAL SOCIETAL SECTOR'S CRUCIAL VITAL ROLE

As interpreted here, the cultural category has a relatively restricted role, including only those societal agencies supplying more or less formal educational assistance. The more formal kind is represented by the schools, extending from lowest to highest academic levels. Specialized institutions and groups engaging in research and its dissemination comprise the less formal sort. Talcott Parsons, the late eminent sociologist, shows how these cultural units make profound communal contributions, what he terms ''pattern maintenance.'' This involves inculcating the values and norms that promote the participants' personal and communal stable unity.[37] The family, he says, also shares this critically important socializing formational duty, but on a very individualized, hence limited, scale. ''Kinship . . . is the substructure of the pattern-maintenance system that operates at the farthest remove from considerations of general culture,'' he tells us.[38]

The cultural concept presently used accordingly reflects the second Vatican Council's distinction of a "sociological sense." It does not emphasize pluralistic, historical aspects as the Council does, however, but unifying metaphysical features.[39] Also like the Council, culture's immediate significance has a rich intellectual and moral or spiritual content. As the Council tellingly indicates,

> . . . when man gives himself to the various disciplines of philosophy, history and of mathematical and natural science, and when he cultivates the arts, he can do very much to elevate the human family (sic) to a more sublime understanding of truth, goodness, and beauty. . . . In this way, the human spirit, being less subjected to material things, can be more easily drawn to the worship and contemplation of the Creator.[40]

There we have succinctly stated culture's crucial import: the enlightening educational services provided by that essential societal sector. Those typical benefits carry both natural and supernatural value, when culture is properly understood, through a "profound inquiry into the meaning of culture and science for the human person."[41] Some comments of Pope Pius XI in his encyclical on Christian Education apply here:

> . . . men . . . realize today more than ever, amid the most exuberant material progress, the inadequacy of earthly goods to produce true happiness either for individuals or for the nations. Hence they feel more keenly in themselves the impulse toward a perfection that is higher. . . . This perfection they seek to acquire by means of education. . . . In fact . . . education consists essentially in preparing man for what he must be and for what he must do here below, that he may attain the sublime end for which he was created.[42]

The "profound inquiry" which the Council mentions thus discloses culture's characteristic role for society, namely, discovering and disseminating truth. Correlating such critical responsibility with Christ's corresponding concentration upon truth's central human relevance, we understand better His transcending attitude toward the family.

Although the latter rightly is seen as sharing in human nature's mediating, formational or "pattern maintenance" dynamic, alongside the cultural counterpart, its pertinent part entails more heavily weighted corporeal, individualizing benefits proportionate to the spiritual, personalizing kind. This still permits some significant, higher-level contributions, since the body represents spirit's supplementary or extended vitalizing influence.[43] The "two in one flesh" relationship and the progeny it begets are far from fostering the temporally and spatially transcendent status that Christ's universalizing outlook and output require. Being "begotten from above," through thoroughly adopting the Word of God as proffered by the Church, transforms individuals and groups into true persons and communities. They then become ever more spiritually vitalized. Hence others ". . . do not know whence (they) come or where (they) go. . . ."[44] "Whoever does the will of my Father . . ." comprise their kin.[45]

The ecclesial religious impact on political relations affords us a very prominent example along the latter lines. While always retaining at least an elementary loyalty toward "homeland," dedicated Christians increasingly emphasize supernatural religious relationships over natural political ones. Rendering Caesar his due gradually contracts specifically before the superior obligation and inclination of becoming "perfect as your heavenly Father," so promoting greater justice and charity among enemies and friends less restrictedly albeit responsibly or proportionately. Due grateful connections with a particular civil community never properly decline entirely during one's earthly sojourn. Comprehensively considered, however, the balance between commitments inclines sharply on the supernatural religious and an accompanying international political side.

Christ's own personal example in surmounting familial ties

throughout His public life is especially illuminating here. The constant ministering by word and attendant deeds in a close friendly circle demanded breaking off all but minimal domestic association. His critical remarks regarding the reason behind a steady concentration upon teaching through parables shows how strong temporal corporeal bonds hamper spiritual insight and involvement. "I use parables when I speak to them," He said, "because they look but do not see, they listen but do not hear or understand."[46] Contrarily, the disciples were praised and rewarded because they had broken, more than less, the heavily bodily familial links. "To you has been given a knowledge of the mysteries of the kingdom of God. . . ."[47] Climaxing earlier efforts at elevating human relations above the decidedly corporeal domestic level by stressing the spiritual even there—"rather (than the bearing womb and nourishing breast) blessed are they who hear the word of God and keep it"—He transferred His mother to the disciple John.[48]

As explained earlier, the present cultural concept refers to those organizations concerned mainly with formal educational services. They accordingly are the societal agencies, academic and similar kinds, that principally satisfy humans' need for continuing truthful formation. This crucial contribution does not stem solely from such professional institutions. Like all fundamental developmental traits characterizing human nature, their apt advancement entails proportionate assistance by other typical collective units. That elementary reinforcing interaction reflects humanity's essential integrity, projected on the societal-communal plane. The cultural combinations' superior status here is a consequence of their especially comprehensive truth-bearing provisions, measured against the remaining comparable human groupings. As we have seen, cultural associations really, albeit partly, represent society's basic maturing effects, whereby the members' inherent spiritual resources become more thoroughly activated. The progress thus achieved at this mediate dynamic level (means, ''pattern-maintenance,'' formational) balances corresponding, yet less consolidated, gains accomplished in the prior, or major, religious dynamic sector (ends, ''goal attainment,'' finalizing). Both fundamental developments simultaneously stimulate related advances amid the essentially subsequent, proportionately minor fine arts' dynamic sphere (methods, ''technological system,'' functional). Those growing benefits on society's spiritual side obviously influence the latter's corporeal, temporal intrinsic divisions, as political, familial, and mundane arts, respectively.[49]

The ultimate, truthful, enlightening, and empowering services that Christ supplies continue to flow chiefly through the Church He established for that enduring officially mediating role. Being His principal societal agency, such religious institution channels supernaturally and naturally saving aid, spiritual-moral, into society's other typical realms: political, cultural, familial, fine and mundane arts. It does so along both personal-individual and communal-societal lines. The latter comprise the main advantages because more directly promoting the greater comprehensive common good. Recall Christ's pertinent statement mentioned previously, when He told the disciples how they would do works ''greater than (His).'' Since surely none could surpass His works of a personal-individual kind, He must have meant their labors associated with organizing and operating the Church. Confronting the various moral-spiritual issues affecting the membership (and others) in the several societal sectors certainly is something Christ seldom did. He did, though, lay the foundations and erect the framework, as it were, keeping His agents closely connected to Him while developing the Church, aided by the Holy Spirit. This foundation and framework principally follows from His messianic message's essential meaning as ''the way, the truth, and the life.'' Adequately understood, the said summary outlines Christ's fundamental mediating import for humans, naturally and supernaturally or creating and redeeming, on both a personal-individual and a communal-societal basis.

Christ's messianic role, perfectly exemplifying human nature's true constitutional and dynamic balance, does not derive mainly from His own share therein, uniquely exalted though that be. Rather is it founded upon His divine nature, substantially united with the human counterpart, as the Church teaches.[50] So eternally existing, He expresses a distinctly equal relation (Son-Word) to the other divine Persons, again as the Church teaches.[51] Such teaching further explains this personal relationship as a "mediating" one, analogically at least, proceeding from the Father and jointly spirating the Holy Spirit. Christ's stated earthly mission—showing humans the way of truth insuring life—consequently represents His divine Trinitarian status, really if remotely. On the latter level, He "mediates" the eternal truth, which "defines" the Father's life, and concomitantly "discloses" the Holy Spirit's diverse responses thereto, again at least analogically. Karl Rahner indicates how the immanent Trinity also is the "economic" (creating) Trinity; hence the Son-Word continues His "mediating" contributions then.[52] When thus acting, He principally provides human nature, the middle creaturely class (mediating between angelic and physical-biologic types), with characteristic capacities for the truth that fosters their refracting the Father's life, aided by the Holy Spirit's practical promptings (way). Human nature's essential resources therefore chiefly reflect a created participation in the Son-Word's infinite personal "mediating" reserves. Such sharing supplies humanity's developmental potentials, what we term the common good. This inherent dynamism exerts its impact most elementally at the individual-personal vital level, and most thoroughly on the societal-communal plane. So collectively organized, the human common good best mirrors the Son-Word's creative role in the divine community or Trinity.

If Christ's crucial mediating formula is appropriately interpreted, then, the middle term (truth) accordingly represents more exactly His "mediating" status amid the divine Trinity. The connection with the logically prior term (life) similarly shows His divine responding relation to the Father; while the conjunction with the logically subsequent term (way) denotes His inspiring relation to the Holy Spirit. Understood in its human societal context, that "mediating" divine role of Christ entails main or determining emphasis upon the mediate structural societal sector: cultural-familial. The prior purposeful sector (religious-political) correspondingly exercises a properly guiding or directing influence, as the subsequent procedural sphere (fine arts–mundane arts) does proportionately along complementary completing lines. Naturally and supernaturally, cultural-familial agencies thus supply the critical consolidating or structuring services most pertinent to human nature's middle creaturely state.

As explained earlier, those dynamic societal interactions occur primarily on humanity's spiritual side, when aptly activated, principally through Christ's revelatory import. They extend from there into the relevant corporeal counterparts. The Church's characteristic supernaturalizing societal contributions (moral-spiritual), as constituting Christ's chief communal representative, consequently are correctly concerned mainly with assisting the mediate societal institutions (cultural) in devising true educational standards for development (teaching). Then it is most comprehensively united to Christ in His most typical mediating human relationship: forming, structuring. The prior, more elemental, sacramental servings (praying, preaching) rather reflect Christ's comparatively indirect human connection: finalizing, guiding or "defining" the Father. Likewise, the subsequent, more supplemental, practically concentrated services (applying the benefits of the sacramental and educational aids) largely display Christ's additional, less direct human involvement: functional, completing, or "disclosing" the Holy Spirit.

Objectively or spiritually considered, therefore, the cultural sector stands essentially superior to the familial in the mediate societal sphere; as the religious sector relates to the political at the major societal level; and the fine arts balance the mundane arts on the minor societal plane. A truly Christian communal order accordingly accentuates its cultural combinations' role over the familial one, thereby emulating Christ's example naturally and supernaturally, or creating and redeeming. As stated at this study's start, however, the said essential balance between the cultural and familial realms frequently becomes disrupted, under human nature's acquired disorderly tendencies. A spiritually subverted cultural secularism will compel Christian and similar supernaturally oriented families to take such corrective, collective action as will effectively protect and promote true human values, personal and communal.[53]

NOTES

1. "Decree on Priestly Formation," n. 16, in *The Documents of Vatican II*, W.M. Abbott, S.J., ed. (New York: America Press, 1966), p. 452. Excerpts from *The Documents of Vatican II* are reprinted with permission of American Press, Inc., 106 West 56th Street, New York, NY 10019.

2. "Dogmatic Constitution on Divine Revelation," n. 24, Ibid., p. 127.

3. Ibid., n. 18, p. 123.

4. Ibid., n. 20, p. 124.

5. Ibid., n. 8, p. 116.

6. John 16:12–14.

7. "Pastoral Constitution on the Church in the Modern World," n. 48, in Abbott, op. cit., p. 250.

8. Ibid., footnote 158, p. 251.

9. Pope Pius XI, "Christian Marriage," in *Social Wellsprings*, J. Husslein, S.J., ed. (Milwaukee: Bruce, 1942), vol. II; nn. 15, 21, 125. Reprinted by permission of the publisher.

10. Pope Paul VI, *Humanae Vitae* (New Haven, Conn.: Knights of Columbus edit., 1968), n. 4, p. 3.

11. Ibid., n. 25, p. 14.

12. Ibid., n. 29, p. 15.

13. Pope John Paul II, "The Community of the Family," n. 13. *The Pope Speaks* 27, no. 1, (1982): 10.

14. Ibid., n. 20, pp. 16–17.

15. Ibid., n. 21, p. 18.

16. Ibid., n. 26, p. 22.

17. Ibid., n. 44, p. 38.

18. Ibid., n. 54, pp. 45–46.

19. Ibid., n. 59, p. 49.

20. John 3:6.

21. 1 Cor. 15:46.

22. H. De Lubac, S.J., *The Splendour of The Church*, M. Mason, trns. (Glen Rock, N.J.: Paulist, 1963), pp. 93–95.

23. J. Fuchs, S.J. and H. Rechter, S.J., *Natural Law*, J. Dowling, trns. (Dublin: Gill & Sons, 1965), pp. 176–177.

24. Matt 5:17—". . . I have come, not to abolish (the law), but to fulfill . . ."

25. John 17:21. As a note to this statement, the *New American Bible* says: "The world is once more to be challenged by the mission of the disciples and given the opportunity of self-judgment inasmuch as it will either accept or reject Jesus."

26. John 3:3–5.

27. Aquinas, *Summa Theologica*, I, Q. 76, A.1, ad. 5; III, Q. 85, A. 1, ad. 4.

28. John 8:32.

29. John 4:24.

30. John 14:6.

31. Aquinas, op. cit., I, Q. 77, A. 2.

32. John 17:17, 19—"Consecrate them by means of truth—Your word is truth. . . . I consecrate myself for their sake now, that they may be consecrated in truth."

33. "Constitution on the Church in the Modern World," nn. 11–39, in Abbott, op. cit., pp. 209–236.

34. John 14:12.

35. Matt. 10:24–25—"No pupil outranks his teacher . . . the pupil should be glad to become like his teacher."

36. "Constitution on the Church in the Modern World," Pt. II, in Abbott, op. cit., pp. 249–289.

37. Parsons, *Social Systems and the Evolution of Action Theory*, pp. 194–195, 254–255.

38. Ibid., p. 195.

39. "Constitution on the Church in the Modern World," n. 53, in Abbott, op. cit., p. 259.

40. Ibid., n. 57, p. 263.

41. Ibid., n. 61, p. 268.

42. Pope Pius XI, "Christian Education of Youth," in Husslein, op. cit., nn. 6–7. Cf. "Declaration on Christian Education," n. 2, in Abbott, op. cit., pp. 640–641.

43. Rahner, "The Theology of the Symbol," pp. 245–249.

44. John 3:8.
45. John 12:49–50.
46. Matt. 13:13.
47. Matt. 13:11.
48. Luke 11:28. John 19:26–27.
49. C. Dawson, *Religion and the Rise of Western Culture*, pp. 12–21.
50. Rahner, *The Teachings of the Catholic Church*, S.J., editor, G. Stevens, trns. (New York: Alba House, 1967), pp. 153–158.
51. Ibid., pp. 92–97.
52. Rahner, *Foundations of Christian Faith*, pp. 135–137.
53. Pope John Paul II, op. cit.,, nn. 8, 40, pp. 6–7, 35–36.